Blowing The Trumpet
In
Open Court

Blowing The Trumpet In Open Court:

Prophetic Judgement And Liberation

Boykin Sanders

Africa World Press, Inc.

P.O. Box 1892
Trenton, NJ 08607

P.O. Box 48
Asmara, ERITREA

Africa World Press, Inc.

P.O. Box 1892
Trenton, NJ 08607

P.O. Box 48
Asmara, ERITREA

Copyright © 2002 Boykin Sanders

Second Printing 2003

Book design: Jonathan Gullery
Cover design: Ashraful Haque

Library of Congress Cataloging-in-Publication Data

Sanders, Boykin
  Blowing the trumpet in open court : prophetic judgement and Liberation / by Boykin Sanders.
    p.cm.
  Includes bibliographical references and index.
  Contents: Listening to the oppressed -- Bombings in Africa: what does it mean? -- The quest for a primordial construct -- Facing up in exile: African reality in the United States -- Facing up at home: negotiating for a future -- The nature of African freedom in America.
  ISBN 0-86543-971-0 -- ISBN 0-86543-972-9 (pbk.)
    1. African Americans--Politics and government. 2. African Americans--Social conditions. 3. African Americans--Civil rights--History 4. United States--Race relations. 5. Blacks--Africa--Politics and government. 6. Blacks--Africa-Social conditions. 7. Colonies--Africa--History. 8. Africa--Colonization--History. 9. Africa--Race relations. 10. National liberation movements--Africa--History. I. Title.

E185.615 .S25 2003
  305.896--dc21   2001004341

To Christa,

and to Minerva in Memoriam

Contents

Preface

For more than forty years social and public policy engineers have focused on creating an indivisible America. The Civil Rights Movement of 1950s and 60s and the Human Rights Movement of the 1970s and 80s were the first installments toward that end. The former – a project of liberal white economic interest and black bourgeois desire – was preparatory, stressing the end of privileges in America based on skin color. The latter (the Human Rights Movement) quantified the former, stressing opportunities for training and economic advancements long denied Africans in America and other disaffected groups. Thus, with a citizenry crossing racial, gender, and class lines that benefited from and gloated in a one-America dream – i.e., an integrated society where race does not determine opportunities – America in the 90s turned to creating an indivisible world in its own image. Not only did America become the world's policeman, enforcing its brand of human rights and freedom; it became a globetrotting missionary, demanding civil and human rights performances, American style, of those seeking America's assistance and beneficence.

So enthralled was America in re-creating the world in its own image that those brooking opposition occasionally found themselves on the list of undesirables. In the name of harmony at home and cooperation abroad America's federal agencies were endowed with increased powers to rein in global dissenters of the American way. On the foreign front the 90s saw stiffening American resolve against governments and peoples whose own domestic agenda disagreed with U.S. policy; e.g., Libya, Iran, Iraq, and Cuba. These were singled out for lengthy U.S. sanctions. On the home front the government instituted policies that spawned more prisons for incorrigibles, more blatant exhibits of one kind of justice for the poor and another for the rich, more forgiveness of age-old sins, and more efforts to kill affirmative action initiatives. And more capital punishment was meted out for the unwanted.

However, those who fell victim to U.S. foreign and domestic objectives did not always roll over on command. This was clearly evinced in cases ranging from Iraq's resistance to U.N. inspections to disaffected militia groups in the U.S.; from confederate flag protesters to low-level insurgency warriors against U.S. supported dictatorships; from anti-American demonstrations abroad to voter disaffection at home. In each instance suppressed and oppressed voices registered concerns, whether in the form of suicide bombings in Israel, farm takeovers in Zimbabwe, or labor strikes in America. Hitherto silent voices begged to be heard.

This text serves as a forum for those disallowed voices. It assumes that the fixed and highly managed forum for public opinion that parades as a people's forum or town meeting in America seldom incorporates average voices. As a person, often idealistic to say the least, I find this repressive – even disquieting – because a few have the last (and too often the only) word on matters affecting the majority. This is unfortunate since no one voice or group of voices on planet Earth can presume to speak fully and satisfactorily about everything for everyone. The truth is that we can speak only about what we know – no more, no less. As such, this text is a project in world-enlarging and room-making. It is about openness to culture "otherness" in a world regulated by one-culture perspectives.

If there is a constitutive or ideological premise that drives this work's purpose, it is this: *Integration made the African world in America voiceless, powerless, and meaningless. It is per-*

haps the greatest mistake Africans in America ever made by their own commission. Integration destroyed the African traditions of self-reliance and independence that were endemic to the African self-understanding of freedom and meaningful existence. As such, it brought great suffering to African people in the U.S., as neocolonial objectives did on the African continent. I postulate here that integration will increase the troubles of African people - barring a change of direction. In order to make a change of direction likely to save the black world, the recapture of its ancestral wisdom, critically and spiritually applied, is essential.

This book discusses the plagues of the African world in a dialogical tenor, making judgments about African missteps while offering a deliverance route based on ancestral wisdom. Born and reared, as I was, in a social context wherein racial designation was expected to determine futures, I learned early on to read and interpret life's printouts. On a different plain, I found my perceptions, judgments, and actions were perennially at war against forces that did not wish me well. These were forces that sought to remove from me the last driblets of my particularity, that is, to erase me from the face of the earth altogether. However, in the end, these forces birthed determination in me. Not only did they anchor my springs of ancestral hope in deadening winters; they kept me sufficiently suspicious of and outside of mainstream pursuits. Thus, I developed a passion for reinstalling the good that was often forgotten or rejected.

Perhaps it is unconventional to thank adverse winds in a venture such as this, in particular those that oppose our quest for the best in the least. Had it not been for such adversaries my concern, respect, and passion for the useful life might not have crystallized in the fashion described here. I would have found myself at the border, crossing over from segregation to integration without second thoughts about what I was doing. Indeed, these adverse winds caused me to rethink life and its purpose. It is because of them I came to think of the future as the past.

Equally important in the shaping of my thoughts and

action processes incorporated in this book are those who encouraged me in friendship and cared about me in dejection. If it had not been for their willingness to stir me beyond disquieting moments, my passion for life in collective terms would not have been fueled. Here belong my living-dead ancestors, my deceased wife Minerva, and our daughter Christa Elise, who could be within the stream of mainstream players but seems more comfortable outside. To them I dedicate this work. Here also belong my colleagues at Virginia Union University Samuel Dewitt Proctor School of Theology under the leadership of Dr. John Kinney and my present and past students who allowed New Testament studies to be nontraditional and relevant. All in one way or another helped to shape my thinking. I am grateful.

In a separate category of thanks without comparison belong the late Dr. Louis C. Brown, M.D., of Atlanta and the late Dr. Herbert O. Edwards, Ph.D., of Baltimore and Durham. Dr. Brown's spiritual depth and brilliance keeps on keeping on. The quietness of Dr. Edwards' commiseration with me about justice and freedom in a collective sense transcends his translation. Neither one could hold his peace in dry and uncertain seasons regarding the African experience in America and throughout the world. Both men lived outside the camp.

Dr. Riggins Earl, a professor of Ethics and Theology at the Interdenominational Theological Center of Atlanta, belongs here too. He kept me in mind out of love for the brethren and out of shared circumstances of common plights and journeys.

Then I thank people across the globe for their role in shaping the contents of this book. They helped me enormously with divine truths and divine ways. In their ordinariness they showed me the way of embodied wisdom and the higher life. They kept my feet and hands steady when less than noble aims and ways could have supplanted what I knew to be right.

Last but not least I want to thank Mr. Kassahun Checole, publisher and editor of Africa World/Red Sea Press, whose openness to voices of the oppressed in the publishing business issued into this book. Without him and his staff this book may not have seen the light of day.

Boykin Sanders
Rembert, South Carolina
November 2001

Introduction

The civil and human rights movements in America and the battles for freedom and independence in Africa from the 1950s through the 1970s produced troubling results in the continental and diaspora African worlds. Traditions that gave Africans distinctiveness and stature in the eyes of peoples and cultures around the world, especially in their own struggles for freedom and their empathy and solidarity with others seeking it, disappeared within a generation. Instead of a freedom-fighting and freedom-embracing spirit, habits that suggest reactionary ways mushroomed within African worlds. In the United States, for example, class concerns overwhelmed ethnic and "third world" matters as issues of importance. On the African continent, concerns, spawned by a long history of colonization, turned into opportunistic endeavors reminiscent of colonial values. Instead of freedom spawning communal solidarity and liberation from Europe and European styles of governance that were pervasive in colonial days, freedom in postcolonial Africa generated an uncritical acceptance of European ways and the shunning of African traditional ways; in both contexts, freedom for Africans meant re-enslavement.

In America, freedom meant job security and promotion in the very world from which the African ancestors fought so long and hard to free themselves; it meant an exodus from African worlds to promise lands controlled and managed by white people. Freedom meant the loss of African independence.

These marked shifts in the continental and dispersion contexts affected African worlds in negative ways. They brought an end to a long-tested principle of African life and survival around the world: *I am because we are, and we are because I am.* That principle, a defining one for the African concept of community in traditional society and a staple for African behavior, was replaced by individualism, i.e., the right of each person to determine life's courses without threat of group sanctions. As a result, a freedom that once suggested interethnic solidarity now suggested individuated existence. In practice the latter meant abandoning African causes and African communities for opportunities and projects in a non-African context.

Guided by the idea that the white world has what the black world needs, a culture of de-Africanized existence has been in the works for more than forty years in African worlds across the globe. In America, Africans made a conscious effort to become more involved in and connected to Euro-American dreams and aspirations. At the same time they became less involved in issues of traditional African communities. Like mainstream priests and priestesses, who ignored the victim of the ditch, Africans today are generally alienated from one another and from their ancestors' focus. Imbued with the market considerations of Western capitalism (losses and gains), Africans of means tend to disregard the battered and bruised of African worlds in quest of personal wealth and fame in white worlds. Thus, those who were oppressed only a few years earlier are now exhibiting behaviors of those they once considered the oppressor.

This book invites readers to reflect critically on these developments in African worlds after some forty years of wilderness wandering in what I believe has been a road of misjudgments in freedom. Here I do not shy away from the consequences of those misjudgments: The African decision to travel the road of integration destroyed Africans and African worlds in America, and it will destroy African distinctiveness and abilities in the post-apartheid South Africa. Here I write this out of conviction: Because of miscalculations in the result of freedom, Africans on the continent and in America are essentially a destroyed people socially, religiously, mentally, spiritually, emotionally, morally, educationally, and economically.

I do not believe that the African situation is irreversible however. My belief is that nations and people can move beyond destructive behaviors if they honestly face up to them, devise ways and means for overcoming them, and commit themselves to programs of alternative histories based on gained insights. For that reason this undertaking is a personal call to duty, following my own journey of more than forty years of African setbacks as well as my opportunities to assist in the work imagining a different future for Africans and African worlds.

It is because of my personal call to duty that I challenge readers of African descent in particular to face up to the realization that something has gone wrong in African worlds. Focusing on what that "something" might be may provoke the usual tendency to side with social scientists in their litany of things that ail the black world: the absence of strong family values, drugs, high unemployment, racism, AIDS, welfare, crime, to name a few. Conservative commentators postulate that these behaviors belong to those who are nonmainstream in outlook and of low intelligence. They say black people, especially those of the underclass, are by nature destructive. For these scientists such behaviors will continue since blacks that participate in them lack the intellectual capacity to move beyond them. More liberal commentators counter that such behaviors can be altered if such groups were offered opportunities in the mainstream. One provocative statistic shows that those who moved from welfare to work in America have become more productive citizens and supports the liberal perspective.

However, what is problematic in both assessments is focus. Both camps focus on symptoms and band-aid solutions rather than on the deep illnesses in African worlds. Their research methods and goals allow them to address symptoms, but not cures. This is because the role of social scientists in America is to advise the government and other agencies on how to stabilize the sick and stay in business, not on how to cure them and go out of business. For that reason my proposal is quite simple: *The gaunt appearance of Africans in America today is rooted in a disease called integration. The gaunt appearance of Africans on the continent is rooted in a disease called neocolonial behavior. It is these diseases that are causing widespread disabilities in African worlds.*

Using the journeyman's genre the first two chapters of this book present a case for changes that move Africans away from painful experiences caused by these diseases to a future without them. I argue that African people have failed the world over and have failed the world because they embrace Western values. These values (global in nature) do not allow for other thinking, other voices, and other plans, only for imperial ones. In the quest to rectify an unacceptable situation, I not only focus on the heavy hearts of the unheard who beg to differ with the status quo; I venture into what might seem ludicrous. Unheard or sideline players participate in discussions that movers and shakers view as their domain alone. These players launch a nonimperial way of thinking about the world and its issues.

Thus, Chapter One challenges those of mainstream orientations – those plotters for "the others" of this world – to listen for once to people for whom they presume to speak. My view is that the voices of nonmainstreamers (nonintegrationist voices) should be heard for the simple reason that the voice that is usually heard is stifling and oppressive, if not corrupting. Accordingly, readers will meet here and there figures in the service of a deconstruction-reconstruction effort vis-à-vis the world, as we know it. Such figures and voices are not fictitious. They force us to see what happens when we tune into stations playing music in a different key.

To that end my deconstruction-reconstruction effort begins in Chapter One "Listening to the Oppressed." Sparked by the U.S. bombings in the Sudan and Afghanistan in August of 1998, this chapter questions and moves away from the "failed states" thesis some Western experts use to account for the presence of those disparagingly called "terrorists." Thus, the questions of our voices: Are people whom Americans call "terrorists" by-products of failed governments? Do they by nature hate Americans, American success, and American democracy?

The 1995 bombing of the Oklahoma federal building assists us with those issues. It opens a channel for so-called "terrorists" to communicate their issues and desires to the world. I argue that if America would only hear what "terrorists" are saying, it would not view them as fanatics who hate "freedom-loving peoples," but as normal people who want freedom and justice too. I argue that the way to solve the problem is to solve the problem about which these "terrorists" complain. The 1994 Zapatista Rebellion in Southern Mexico illustrates my point. But I wonder can we move forward in this debate before putting ourselves in the position of those charged?

Chapter Two, "Bombings in Africa: What Does It Mean?" invites readers to reflect on the 1998 bombings in East Africa in view of the suggestions of Chapter One. I propose that the bombings in Kenya and Tanzania were more than U.S. embassy bombings. Africans and other voiceless people speak of indifference to or moving away from African values and the need for atonement in African societies. Here I argue that Africa's shift away from African values is Africa's way of negotiating neocolonial mistakes. The chapter offers non-European, heretofore voiceless speakers a forum to speak about African concerns and perceptions ignored by the Western world. Perhaps the musings and reflections of these voiceless ones will be seen as a challenge to Europeans to incorporate more than what is brought to bear on the interpretation of matters involving non-Europeans. In any case, they set the stage for the primer idea of this book – that integration and integrationist behaviors destroyed Africans and African worlds in America.

Chapters Three to Six lift the lid off the African world in the service of exposing forty years of mistakes. These chapters pinpoint where African worlds went wrong and continue to go wrong, but I do not place blame for mistakes within African worlds where it is usually placed – at the doorsteps of white folks. Rather I place blame at African doorsteps, since for more than forty years the misuse and abuse of privileges in freedom were African decisions and undertakings. My position in these chapters is anchored in ancestral views and therefore anticipates my suggestions in Chapter Seven, "African Freedom and Liberation in America."

My view is elementary: As Africans created the world they now inhabit, they must become architects and designers of different African worlds if there is to be a different (and better) African world in the future. For me this perspective is a down payment on African redemption. Of course, I am aware that such a view runs counter to those of integrationist strategists in the United States and now in South Africa and neo-colonial Africa.

Chapter Three, "The Quest for a Primordial Construct," chronicles my search for meaning in an African world which was on its way to the bombings I discuss in Chapter Two. Driven by my own growing uneasiness with the African drift towards disaster in America, I chronicle not only the manner of this drift and its impact on me but my way of dealing with it. This chapter relates my personal quest for stability through nonintegrationist means in America that brought me, through my studies, to the African alternative way. This chapter relates how I literally read myself into an imagined exodus from the lapsing integrationist-mad world around me and how I sought to ensure my future by making rounds in Africa through the knowledge I had gained. This chapter describes my quest for an African oasis in Africa, since the African life and culture of my segregated, protected world in the American south was disappearing before my very eyes. In all honesty my description of a fallen African world delineated in Chapter Six began years before, in the early seventies when I sensed that the holy and solid ground of my sacred world was being devoured by the squalor of Babylon (America); but primordial Africa had cracks as well.

Chapter Four discusses how changes under integration made Africans in America bards of Euro-American confinement camps. Under the title "Facing Up in Exile: African Reality in the United States," I reminisce about the willful decision Africans in America made to leave their own turf of self-definition, self-culture, and self-reliance in the 1960s for worlds organized, managed, and determined by white Americans. As a result, the primordial idea – *I am because we are, and we are because I am* – became less operative and determinative for African behavior in America. A people believing in solidarity and communal responsibility became individualistic and opportunistic. Success no longer meant holding out together; rather it meant positions, promotions, and acquisitions in Euro-American worlds. Chapter Four concludes with my response to this trend: I became a rebel for *a life on the other side of the river.* As a result of my consistent and unbending actions over the years, I became a resister.

It was as a resister, however, that I began my journey home. I needed something other than the destruction of African people, something more lasting. I did not think it proper to cave in and give up, and so I rallied for the long haul through techniques of self-expression and self-determination. Nevertheless, were my efforts fruitless since, as I believed, the African situation in America had already moved beyond rescue? Or had it?

These questions led me to a quest for self-validation – the thing I needed most as life in America was wearing me down. I needed to live for and struggle on behalf of a life I considered worthy a little while longer, and so I turned to Africa to gather what I was missing in America. Chapter Five presents that story and its results. Dubbed "Facing Up at Home: Negotiating for a Future," this chapter tells the story of sad truths in Africa: Colonialism and its harvest extractions had virtually destroyed continental Africans. I mused that Africa held a shine only for diaspora Africans, not for continental ones. I reasoned that traditional culture is either denied or abandoned by continental Africans. This chapter discusses why this is the case.

Three writers join me to discuss this anomaly of my continent. The last of the three finds little about which to be hopeful there. His words are depressing, blunt, and gripping. In the end, they are graphically frank and realistic. But are they final for Africa? At sunset our thoughts shift. By exhortatory means I turn to images of a reconfigured and reconstructed Africa after so much sadness and gloom. Thus, the epitaph for Africa is shaped by a single question: Can Africa live again?

In Chapter Six, "The Nature of African Freedom in America," I write frankly about African blunders in freedom in America. I magnify my thesis, noting that freedom for Africans in America under integrationist terms consists of doing what *is viewed as independence in the white world* rather than *doing what needs to be done for the black world*. I assert that freedom, as integrationist opportunities, became for the African middle class a smorgasbord of ostentatious desire and nonprincipled conduct and living. For this class, in most instances, it meant acquiring many times over the needs of a lifetime. It meant leaving the masses behind and serving as buffers between black and white worlds. It meant shelving a sense of morality in a world of plenty. It meant an opportunity to become attached to systems made by others rather than to a commitment shaped by the needs of the African masses.

I propose that freedom of this type is destructive. Since African philosophy invites us to question events and their manifestations in the world, then one might ask why the African landscape in America is so decimated today? Our dialogue closes with a query: Where do we go from here?

Chapter Seven, "African Freedom and Liberation in America," concludes our discussion. We offer a new definition of freedom as guide for African existence in America today. Rather than a chance to crow about individual accomplishments, I advocate ethnic cooperative endeavors. Ethnic solidarity is black power and salvation in a world of winds tempered by racial hostility against people of African descent. I show that freedom constructed in this fashion is endemically African, useful and salvific for future African worlds. Surprisingly this kind of freedom is touted by no less a figure than Paul the apostle, a man once ridiculed as unhelpful to Africans in their pursuit of justice and freedom in America.

In closing our conversation I call for no less than a restructured existence in African America based on group solidarity principles. Such an existence would be guided by prophetic spirituality. Prophetic existence means turning away from that which imperils and dissipates to that which reintroduces the proper life. It is a deconstruction-reconstruction challenge under the auspices of an ancestral blueprint. As such I offer, for starters, seven directives for a life free of current African sins.

The epilogue draws the curtain on this undertaking by recalling what Booker T. Washington said and did more than a century ago when the black people of Alabama had a dream but no finances to assist in its fulfillment. Speaking of the need for new dormitory space for a fast-growing student population at Tuskegee University shortly after emancipation, Washington said: "We knew we could name it, even though we were in doubt about our ability to secure the means for its construction."

My aim here is singular: to propose a future for African worlds in the hope of reversing the situation of African existence today. I seek something better. I assert that integration and neocolonial attitudes and practices have decimated African worlds. What follows is an effort to layout specifics of this tragedy and proposals to remedy it.

Perhaps readers will find some benefit in what I write here. Anything gleaned is of course imperfect, yet we must begin to talk about solving the problems of black worlds and other worlds. If you find anything useful towards that end let it be seasonal at best. I say this because I do not intend to make the mistake of others before me. I want no one to think that what I write or suggest is forever fitting for solving African problems for all times and all seasons. However, in a world where people are searching for something more substantive and stable than postmodern drifting, I am inclined to commend ancestral ways as a means to redeem African worlds. For me, there is a degree of the eternal about them. I am quite certain of this: The African world was better with those ancestral ways than without them. Can you imagine a world totally bereft of them?

CHAPTER ONE

Listening to the Oppressed

On the waterfront in Philadelphia, Pennsylvania, there is a memorial from the city to military personnel who died in the Beirut, Lebanon bombing of 1983. Two hundred and forty-three American marines were killed in that attack. Those from Philadelphia are remembered as follows:

October 23, 1983
243 Servicemen Killed in Beirut
Lebanon Terrorist Bombing
IN MEMORIAM
To the Philadelphia Marine Casualties
of the Beirut Peace Keeping Mission

Listed below this epitaph are the names of the peacekeepers, followed by a challenge to all readers and viewers:

"If you forget my death,
then I died in vain."

Some distance away from the memorial honoring the peacekeepers is another memorial. It is posted to the memory of Christopher Columbus. Sponsored by a group known as the 500 Corporation, this memorial pays homage to "the New World's founding father." It commemorates European ventures in the Western Hemisphere more than 500 years ago.

Christopher Columbus, like the Beirut marine mission or what an Orwellian mindset would arrogantly call "peacekeepers," is remembered in the most favorable of terms. He is charismatic leader, navigator, explorer, visionary, naturalist, mathematician, and cartographer, but there is no memorial to the millions of Native Americans whose freedom, hopes and bodies perished because of his desire to explore and conquer the New World as a free spirit. His freedom-seeking venture meant Native American annihilation.

No real American (native) face can be seen on that waterfront. No Native American voice can be heard there. There are no inscriptions commemorating their noble defenses against invasions of their lands; there are no thoughts from them about life. We neither see nor hear anything from those who flattened the marine barracks in Lebanon. We have no thoughts reflecting their perspectives on the "Peace Keeping Mission." On that front they are not permitted to speak. Viewers of the memorial are only allowed to see America as a just nation – as peacekeepers – and are told how to view those who killed the marines. They are uncivilized barbarians who kill innocent people; they kill peacekeepers. As such the message of the memorial planners is clear: America does not negotiate with terrorists!

This chapter questions the tactic that categorically describes nations and their citizens as terrorists simply because they attack U.S. citizens and institutions. It questions whether this tactic is helpful in solving what America calls "terrorist activities" in the world today. More importantly, it asks whether America and its allies can move beyond the status quo regarding those classified as terrorists by incorporating new voices – unconventional ones – in the discourse on terrorism? It asks whether there might be an open and honest

24

dialogue about this issue and whether nontraditional voices might join the discussion? The final question, then, becomes: Is there room in and beyond America for more than a one-channel voice?

Switching Stations in America

As the month of August is a season for black community revival in South Carolina, the summer of 1998 found me once again a seeker. I was invited to share my views on religion with the Savannah Grove Baptist Church. A season or two before I was often concerned about the nature of revivals in African communities in America and had managed to convince the minister of Savannah Grove, a friend of mine, that we needed a change of direction in black church revival meetings. My reasoning reflected my growing uneasiness that revivals in black church communities had essentially run their course. They had undergone little change since I was a child, yet African communities in America had changed a great deal. African needs were different, but revivals still concentrated on converting the unsaved. In recent years I had witnessed few converts to Christianity during revival sessions, yet black parishioners still attended August revivals in good numbers. Why?

In one conversation with the minister about this issue I suggested that our concern about revivals, vis-à-vis the needs of revival attendees, might perhaps be addressed under what is called Bible Lectures as a feature of the revival at Savannah Grove. Our decision was to devote part of each session to that feature, placing stress on raising and thinking through major issues or tenets in religion for good practical ends. The rest of the session might be devoted to preaching – the traditional expectation of African revivals in America. After some discussion regarding format and style for the Bible Lectures portion of the revival we agreed to initiate our plan at the 1998 community revival. My lectures would take place from 6:30 to 7:30 each evening (five sessions in all), followed by preaching from a guest evangelist.

I was following our new script under the theme "Is

Religion Enough to Save Us?" during an August that seemed unlike any other in America. The people and the media had become obsessed with an American scandal – President Clinton's relationship with an intern. America and the world had been curious about the extent of the relationship since the previous January. The moment of truth had come. On 17 August, President Clinton appeared on national and international television and admitted to having an "inappropriate relationship" with the intern, Monica Lewinsky, virtually guaranteeing the topic of world discussion for a long time to come. As if to concede the point, the President went into seclusion on Martha's Vineyard, but the seclusion was not long.

It was now 18 August. I had been spiritually dejected and in the doldrums since the night before. Television at my hotel was a one-picture show – the Clinton-Lewinsky affair. Not only was I tired of seeing it on television, but, even more so, I was tired of the pervasive self-righteousness throughout America and the world. It seemed so hypocritical. These self-righteous binges were impinging on my time, distracting from my revival responsibilities. So about midday, 18 August, I decided to retire the television altogether.

Television, however, has its own magic. I found myself wondering whether the Clinton-Lewinsky affair was still the featured item in the news? I was particularly interested in features that might have some bearing on the topic I would be discussing the evening of 18 August. So at 4pm I switched on the television to satisfy my curiosity. To my surprise, CNN broadcasters were focusing on quite a different story—U.S. missile strikes against Afghanistan and Sudan, and President Clinton's address to the nation from the White House that evening concerning those strikes. Before long CNN reporters announced that the sites in Afghanistan were terrorist bases and that the one in the Sudan contributed to the production of VX nerve gas. Furthermore, both sites were connected to and supported by Osama bin Laden, a wealthy Saudi Arabian citizen who was much discussed in the media. Osama bin Laden, we were told, was the mastermind behind the 7

August bombings of U.S. embassies in Tanzania and Kenya. In those bombings more than 200 people died including twelve Americans, and scores of others were injured. The Sudanese and Afghan strikes were billed as an America payback for the 7 August bombings.

At 6pm on 18 August, I turned off the television once again and went on to the revival as scheduled. Few at the revival had heard about the missile strikes and so most did not realize the national conversation had suddenly changed. I reasoned that my audience had not heard of this change for the same reason that I almost had not. Perhaps they, too, had boycotted television, because it had become singularly focused on the Clinton-Lewinsky affair. At any rate I was not particularly baffled that my revival audience did not know about the Afghan and Sudanese situation. Perhaps many had never heard of such places.

Returning from the revival around 10:30pm I switched on CNN for the latest on the strikes and found that its focus was not on the expected, i.e., those injured or those killed in Sudan and in Afghanistan. Instead, its focus was on Osama bin Laden, reporting that U.S. intelligence had been watching him for a long time, and that he had used his considerable wealth to finance worldwide terrorist operations against the U.S. Thereafter, the newscaster added that U.S. charges against bin Laden ranged from his suspected involvement in the bombing of the World Trade Center in 1993 to the murder of sixty-two tourists in Egypt in 1997.

Our revival ended that August, but, for me, interest in Osama bin Laden did not. In time he would become an American obsession. We were told that U.S. intelligence had supplied and supported him and Afghan rebels in their war against the Soviet Union in the 1980s, but that he and his followers had now turned against America. We were told that he had pledged to strike U.S. interests the world over. Then we were told that he was involved in activities of the Al-Shifa plant of Khartoum, a plant that reportedly produced VX nerve gas. Later we were told that bin Laden was involved in the October 2000 bombing of the USS Cole in Yemen. And now we are told that bin Laden ordered the 11 September, 2001 hijacking of the planes that were commandeered and crashed into the World Trade Center Towers and the Pentagon.

Osama bin Laden became a wanted man in America. The following profile of him emerged and grew in the minds of Americans and the world:

He is an angry, Islamic maniac.
He is committed to killing U.S. citizens
    anywhere in the world.
He is a terrorist committed to killing innocent people.
He is against freedom and democracy.
He is against the American way of life.
He is foremost among terrorists in the world.

To silence this madman all Americans and their allies were asked to join a worldwide hunt for him. The American government offered two $5 million rewards for information leading to his whereabouts and capture. A U.S. court handed down a 238-count indictment against him.

The U.S. government was now preoccupied with Osama bin Laden. The Taliban leadership of Afghanistan was asked to assist the U.S. in his arrest, the U.S. even threatening Taliban leaders with an economic blockade if they refused to cooperate, and with their destruction if bin Laden was not delivered to American authorities. However, the U.S. media allowed little from bin Laden and his followers. Without comments from them, the U.S. etched an indelible image of bin Laden in the minds of the American people as a killer of the innocent, an uncivilized madman, an indiscriminate killing machine, and a hater of Americans. Is this an accurate portrait of Osama bin Laden and the Afghan and Sudanese people?

Tunes of Different Drummers

The Sudanese ambassador to the United Nations, Elfatih Muhamed Ahmed Erwa, challenged the U.S. position on the 18 August 1998 missile strikes, charging that the U.S. had bombed his country without justification. As to the strikes against the Al-Shifa plant in Khartoum, Erwa disputed both the U.S. contention regarding the purpose of the plant and Sudan's ties with Osama bin Laden. He condemned the strikes as barbaric. According to *USA Today* the ambassador said: "We are going to act within civilized international law and ask the [U.N.] Security Council to look into the matter."[1]

Erwa denied U.S. charges that the Al-Shifa plant produced agents for chemical weapons. He revealed that the plant was opened in 1996. Later, the Associated Press reported that the plant produced about half the country's pharmaceutical products. Others stated that the plant produced about 100,000 liters of veterinary pharmaceutical products for Iraq under an oil-for-food agreement the United Nations had brokered.

Eventually, world opinion would go against the U.S. vis-à-vis the Sudanese complaint. For example, the designer of the plant (a U.S. chemical engineer and a former Merck pharmaceutical corporation employee) corroborated the Sudanese position in a public statement: "We have no evidence or have seen no products, commercial products, that are sold of this facility."[2] In addition, some European "diplomats whose governments supported the raids" later doubted that "Al-Shifa was a proper target...."[3] Eventually, the U.S. became silent on the issue.

So what are we to believe when those maligned and dismissed as enemies seldom figure in public discourse and are unlikely to be granted a hearing by those who manipulate public opinion? What can we learn from individuals and nations that ruling class individuals and governments disparagingly refer to as terrorists? Is there room for voices that make managers uncomfortable?

Switching Channels

If America and its allies hope to get a better reading on those whom the government calls terrorists, one acknowledgement is necessary: The word "terrorist" is political and pejorative. It is not my preference for groups or individuals so classified;

Pejorative - derogatory

I employ it as the generally accepted one for the purpose of this discussion. What I mean is that one person's terrorist is another's saint. One person's maniac is another's freedom fighter.

On the one side of the political divide are those who are under attack by those called terrorists. These people usually assign unsavory motives to their attackers (those so-called terrorists), often neglecting to ask their attackers why. In cases where those who are attacked know why, they are unlikely to state it publicly. On the other side are attackers who are often viewed by supporters and sympathizers in positive terms. Attacks are often viewed in retributive terms. Attackers (and their supporters) tend to view their acts – what the attacked usually call "terrorist crimes" – as a payback for past deeds done against their interest. Here the attackers think of themselves as executioners of an "eye for an eye and a tooth for a tooth" philosophy, to use a biblical analogy. This being the case, attackers hardly think of themselves as malevolent, since in their view they are soldiers of justice or redeemers of defaced honor.

But how are the attacked likely to respond to this position? Not thinking in the terms of those who attack them, the attacked may typecast their attackers as barbarians, as individuals who exhibit behavior unbecoming of humans because their methods of attack are glaring and repulsive. In such an assessment the attacked forget what generated the attack in the first place. This usually occurs because the attacked (in this case the stronger by comparison) usually will not admit that violence is also a justifiable weapon used by the weak (so-called terrorists) to express displeasure with the strong. And to generate public outrage against what might be considered "justifiable acts," the appellation "terrorist" often becomes a political weapon in the hands of the strong to discredit legitimate concerns of the weak. Thus statements from the attacked (the strong) that their attackers hate freedom loving nations and peoples should not be accepted without pause. Such views are often tailored to put attackers in the column of inherent wickedness as the attacked bask in the light of goodness. Questions designed to ascertain why attackers (a.k.a. terrorists) do what they do are generally not allowed to surface simply because managers of public opinion have a vested interest in maintaining the status quo on terrorism. As such, the public comes to depend on the status quo for views on terrorists and terrorism, coached into thinking the worst: Terrorists are hell-bent on killing the innocent, especially freedom-loving white Americans. *Media view*

Terry Scott, a retired Army special operations commander, exhibited this disposition, reacting to the East African bombings in an article by *The Boston Globe* writer Charles Sennott. Of terrorist activities in the last decade of the twentieth century, he offered the following thesis for public consumption:

> What has changed in the last 10 years is a change from politically motivated terrorism to religiously motivated terrorism. And the groups are emerging out of failed states, such as Sudan and Afghanistan, which are attracting transnational, ad hoc groupings.[4]

Professor Richard Shultz of Tufts University Fletcher School of Law adds to this portrait:

> What we see in this case and others is a larger ideological context of Islam against the West. Terrorism is becoming more religious and the roots are therefore more grandiose and less specific and the targeting more random.[5]

Obviously the goal of these commentators was to allay public fears about the relationship between religion and terrorism, a matter that deeply concerned America and its allies because of the increased role Islamic fundamentalists played in Middle East politics in the last ten years. However, one must ask whether the readings of Scott and Shultz should be allowed to stand as stated?

Our Turn, Thank You

That terrorist activities in recent years against the U.S., Israel, and their allies signify an ideological difference with the West cannot be denied, at least for Scott and Shultz. "Terrorists" work against their targets in the name of an ideological divide, especially those that Western sources brand as "Islamic fundamentalists." For example, some fundamentalists of the Middle East have made it quite clear that they engaged in a *jihad* (holy war) against their enemies – usually identified as the U.S. and Israel or, to a lesser degree, European nations. Often viewing themselves as inheritors of centuries-old debates and conflicts between East and West, Mohammed and Jesus, Christianity and Islam, righteousness and unrighteousness, and so on, Islamic adherents and sympathizers often describe the West as inherently corrupt and satanic. Some have been known to refer to America as the Great Satan who must be stopped at any cost. The West is not totally innocent, for it has also fostered opposition to Islam. Crusaders of the Middle Ages, for example, thought of themselves as warriors against Islam "to recover the holy places (Palestine) from the infidels" (Muslims). In more recent times, Christian fundamentalists in the West have not been above showing intolerance for Islam, as well as a disregard for the religious traditions of the Orthodox Christian East since the fall of the Soviet Union. Thus, Scott and Shultz's view that Middle East "terrorists" acts in recent times characterize Islam's difference from the West is quite in synchrony with more ancient and contemporary debates between the two traditions. As Islamists have exhibited hostility toward those who disregard or dismiss their faith and traditions, keepers of Western sacred canons have done the same.

Yossef Bodansky's work on Osama bin Ladin has identified several underlining causes for the present struggle. Indirectly, he points out, the Islamic jihad waged against the U.S. by bin Laden and his supporters seeks extrication of U.S. and Western forces from Islamic holy places and lands.[6] Jihad warriors – Muslim extremists in the eyes of the West – are incensed that U.S. troops are permitted to camp on Saudi soil, holy ground for them. In their view U.S. military personnel (infidels) on Saudi soil is a violation of Sharia (Muslim law), which Muslim fundamentalists view as a great offense against Allah. They take it as their sacred duty to Allah, as true Muslims, to rid their Holy Land (Saudi Arabia) of all pollution (U.S. troops).

Let us examine Scott and Shultz's other claims. Are terrorist targets today less specific, more random, than they were ten years ago as Shultz suggested? Are terrorists less forthcoming about their identity these days, or are "failed states" hatcheries for terrorists as Scott suggests? [Note: Scott seems to suggest that terrorists choose their targets based on envy, i.e., their targets have succeeded at that which terrorists and their supporters have failed. Thus we often hear that terrorists do not like U.S. citizens, U.S. democracy.]

While experts like Scott and Shultz are to be commended for what they offer on the subject, I propose here a slightly different reading of their proposals at several points. First, I would amend Shultz's "less specific" regarding the roots and targets of terrorists to read "specific." His "less specific" changed to "specific" would reverse the view that terrorists have become less resolute about their targets and goals in the last ten years. This emendation would bring flashbacks of the World Trade Center (1993), Khobar Towers (1996), sixty-two tourists in Egypt (1997), U.S. embassies in Tanzania and Kenya (1998), Planet Hollywood in Cape Town, South Africa (1998), Chechen attacks against Russia (1999), countless attacks against Israel, the USS Cole (2000), and the World Trade Center and Pentagon (2001). So, with this emendation Middle East Islamist terrorists are clear about their targets. They target Israel, the U.S., and U.S.-Israeli allies.

Second, I propose that the issue of the identity of so-called terrorists be altered to fit reality. For most U.S. citizens, terrorists are Middle East, non-Christian lunatics; foreigners who are envious of U.S. citizens and their success. For example, if a government building was attacked by stealth in the United States or abroad, U.S. intelligence would usually turn to assign blame to the Middle East. Even in the case of the bombing of the Oklahoma federal building on 19 April 1995, the government first looked eastward for culprits. However, the Oklahoma bombing was not the work of those usually blamed for terrorist activities against U.S. citizens. It was the work of homegrown U.S. citizens. Furthermore, the motive of the bombers was clear: Homegrown citizens believed, rightly or wrongly, that domestic and foreign policy decisions did not honor their concept of America; nor did they honor their own their personal lives. From their government's conduct towards them, they inferred that their government no longer represented their interests, especially in the opportunities and the amenities it offered foreigners but not ordinary citizens like themselves. As such, people like Timothy McVeigh and Terry Nichols declared war on the United States of America, in the belief that their government had failed them.

This allusion brings me to my third point, proposing that Scott's "failed states" thesis is untenable based on several observations. First, it seems improbable that terrorists would vent their rage on *other peoples or governments* for the failings of their own governments. In his statement that "failed states, such as Sudan and Afghanistan" hatch terrorists, Scott proposes that "envy of U.S. citizens and their government" lies behind their desire to attack U.S. citizens and U.S. interests. However, if Oklahoma is an index for terrorist behavior, then a new hypothesis is possible: Hatched terrorists attack those who hatch them. Thus, if the bombers who destroyed the federal building in Oklahoma were hatched in the U.S., then, according to Scott's thesis, the "failed state" is the United States of America.

Another reason to question Scott's thesis is that it assigns no role to the nation or to the people attacked in the creation of terrorists. No blame is allotted to the U.S., or to Kenya or to Tanzania in the bombings of 7 August 1998. Only the Sudan and Afghanistan can be blamed since they are the failed states.

A final reason to question Scott's thesis is that so-called terrorists had no role in creating the thesis. Locked behind the

U.S. "non-negotiation with terrorists" policy, they are voiceless. If terrorists could speak for themselves, we might learn that they refer to themselves as "freedom fighters" rather than as "terrorists" – an offensive appellation that the U.S. and its allies assigned to them.[7]

Hearing the Oppressed

In a society of open dialogue honesty compels us to entertain the possibility that so-called terrorists like Osama bin Laden are not charged with bombing Afghanistan and Sudan. Like the Oklahoma bombers their alleged acts of terrorism apparently were triggered by the view that the people or targets bombed had wronged them in some way. In McVeigh's case the charge was that the U.S. was on the wrong path and needed to change direction. Perceiving for some time that he and his supporters had no voice in public discourse, they did the next best thing: They resorted to warring against those whom they believed denied them their rights and privileges in hopes of garnering public sympathy for the rights they honored. In their minds the U.S. government was to be blamed for their plight, and so the target of their terrorist activity was the United States of America.

The mindset of so-called Middle East terrorists seems no different. For Palestinians a major concern is that Israel, with the backing of the U.S. and some European governments, not only dislodged them from their homes but bar them from returning with full rights to their own land. They are obsessed, according to some analysts, with the fact that Palestinians and Arab nations have been gradually loosing their lands and resources to Israel since 1948 by wars, annexations, and other methods. They are deeply grieved that the U.S. supports Israel's occupancy and annexation policies, appearing unwilling to dissuade Israel from its quest to absorb more of their territory. In their minds the U.S. role in this policy is anachronistic, given that it is the world's policeman for human rights. Thus, like most voiceless peoples who at first engage in gradualist methods to regain lost rights and privileges, [like, for example, the African National Congress

ı - error in chronology, misplacing of persons, events, objects, or customs

35

(ANC) after 1912], many Arabs from Palestine eventually resorted to extreme measures to call attention to their plight. The intifada uprisings of 1982 and 2000-2002 are cases in point. Palestinians have and do register their disdain with Israel for not respecting their rights. They view the U.S. and Israel as co-conspirators against Palestinian and Arab rights.

Osama bin Laden, the most dangerous terrorist alive according to the U.S. government, is perhaps no different in this regard. According to Bodansky, the alleged acts of bin Laden and fellow Muslims are designed to send America a message. Referencing source announcements from groups calling themselves the Liberation Army of the Islamic Sanctuaries and the Islamic Army for the Liberation of Holy Places, Bodansky provided evidence that showed that the alleged "terrorist" actions of bin Laden and his supporters relate to the deep grievances of Arab peoples. Unable to speak to U.S. officials, since the U.S. government neither talks to nor negotiates with terrorists, they speak to the people of America through other means, seeking to convey that U.S. forces are to withdraw "from the Muslim lands in general and the Arabian Peninsula in particular." Furthermore, these armies appeal to the U.S. government to comply with certain demands. One such demand is that the U.S. lifts its naval blockade against Muslim nations in the Persian Gulf. Others are that the U.S. end its support of Israel, end its war "against young Muslims under the pretext of fighting terrorism," leave Muslim waters, and put "an end to the campaigns of extermination conducted by the U.S. against certain Muslim nations under the guise of economic sanctions."[8]

Thus the view from "terrorist" quarters is different. Apparently so-called terrorists of the Middle East are seeking to re-establish full and unhindered access to their holy places and sacred lands by means of a jihad against the U.S. and its supporters. The Zapatista rebellion on New Year's day (1994) in Southern Mexico illustrates this point.

Named for its revolutionary leader, Emiliano Zapata, the 1994 rebellion represented Morelos' Campesino (peasant) Indian outrage against the oppressive tactics of powerful landowners and politicians who had trampled on their rights by taking possession of the land they considered theirs. It grew out of a movement that had sought to awaken Mexico and the world to the plight of Southern Mexico's native population. It grew out of corporate interest systematically violating native Indian rights, especially violations by sugar planters and loggers. These, with non-interference of the government, made lives of the indigenous people miserable through land seizures.

The seizure of Indian land, according to John Womack, Jr., took place through "political and judicial maneuvers – condemnations, court orders, foreclosures, and defective-title ruling,"[9] but the Mexican government would not intercede on behalf of Indian rights. The government paid little or no attention to Indians protesting unjust procedures and violations. As a result, the indigenous Indians would become sharecroppers in the very field they own. Adding insult to injury, as Womack illustrates, the land thieves in some instances would bring in workers to live on the land the conscripts had taken from the rightful owners. When rightful owners (the Indians) protested and resisted, they were stringently rebuffed. Some were jailed. Others found that their water rights were cancelled. Still others had more of their land taken away. Thus land grabbing virtually became a scorched-earth policy or slow genocide against the Indians. The goal was to erase Indians from life and memory in Southern Mexico. Any organized objection against this policy was met with measures designed to compound Indian misery.[10]

With the deep wounds of misery festering, the 1994 uprising was the Indians' way of announcing to Mexico and to the world that they would no long accept the fate to which they were being assigned in Southern Mexico. Believing that they could not receive justice in Mexico, they took matters into their own hands. Jorge Castaneda describes the circumstances that led to the uprising:

> The security force repressed indigenous villages without mercy. They violated human rights, raped

women, jailed leaders and priests, burned villages and hamlets, and failed to address age-old demands. The people of Chiapas...wanted to live with dignity, instead of being humiliated, beaten, and repressed."[11]

For Castaneda the charge that Indians were seeking to overthrow the government was not the cause of the uprising, as ruling class interests had claimed; land violations were.[12]

Thus, in the Chiapas rebellion of 1994, the oppressed Morelos Indians were simply expressing that the Mexican government had to end its support of land grabbers and industrialists at their expense. For these oppressed natives, guerrilla warfare was the only alternative left against a regime that refused to hear their pleas for justice and for democracy, a democracy that allows the voiceless to be heard and, when heard, respected. It was an act of the oppressed seeking freedom from oppressors. It was the work of freedom fighters.

Blowing the Trumpet in Open Court

My contention here is that terrorist voices are simply the voices of the oppressed. With that the contention should end here, except for one final note. Before the dust had settled on the new conversation the Clinton administration had generated via its missile strikes against Afghanistan and Sudan and before the revival session had ended at Savannah Grove that August, a friend called me and raised a most perplexing issue. At least it was perplexing in his mind. He wanted to hear a word or two from me on the difference between the "terrorists" who bombed the U.S. embassies in East Africa and the Ku Klux Klan (KKK) "terrorists" who bomb African churches and homes in America. I noted the seriousness of his concern, but related that I did not usually link the two. He, then, reminded me that both were killers and both hated their victims. In addressing his concern I surmised that KKK violence against its victims was not based on the view that the KKK needed to right a wrong perpetuated against KKK members by the targets of their venom. I thought that KKK terrorist conduct was race-based (against Jews and blacks) and that any members of an ethnic group the KKK finds unacceptable are a potential victim of its ire. Furthermore, I noted that what made Middle East "terrorists" different is that unlike the KKK ire against its victims, their operations were determined not by race- but issue-based concerns.

Middle East "terrorists," I continued, are of the opinion that a right that should have been theirs is systematically violated or denied, and that those who have violated or denied them their rights must cease these violations, disregarding ethnic persuasion or color. Violators might be black, yellow, red, green or any combination thereof. To illustrate the point I noted that some Middle East "terrorists" insist that Israel is denying Palestinians access to their land, and that the U.S. conspires with Israel (and perhaps a whole host of others) in this denial. I stated that "terrorists" believe that their pleas for reversal of misdeeds against them are virtually ignored by Israel and its supporters, and that the United States, in particular, sides with Israel against Palestinian and Arab interests. Concluding that no amount of civil pleading will reverse their dire situation, they resort to suicide bombing and other means in hopes of persuading the U.S., Israel, and their supporters to deal with them justly and fairly.

I told my friend that the situation of terrorists is comparable to a person who daily, but without success, begs another to remove his large foot from his neck. In fact, the more the suppressed victim pleads for relief the harder the violator presses the victim's neck. Exasperated, the victim begins to fight back using any available means – suicide bombings, bomb threats, airplane hijackings, hostage seizures.... I told my friend that terrorism is the way of desperate people looking for relief and justice. I asked him if he could in any way commiserate with them? Could he walk a mile in their shoes?

I indicated to him that I had high hopes that the nightmare of the Middle East would end soon. Once governments and peoples moved to honest and open dialogue, I thought, the causes behind terrorist activities would begin to wane; 'old terrorists' and 'old oppressors' could meet at the table of understanding. I told him such appears to be the case in South Africa now that apartheid is officially ended. But I reminded him that justice is the preamble to peace.

I pleaded that he should enlarge his heart and view "terrorists" as fellow human beings, not as the embodiment of Satan. They are not inherently evil, only people pushed to the edge of despair. I even urged that he would see them as God's children too! They are people who care about freedom as much as any on the face of the earth. I begged my friend to consider them not as terrorists, but as human beings, as freedom fighters, and as people who desire what all human beings want.

I told him that Palestinians are not latter-day conquistadors; they didn't seem interested in land grabbing or suppression of rightful owners. They did not seem to want what belongs to others. They just wanted what belongs to them.

I then urged that he would seek a deeper understanding of what he called "excesses in barbarity of terrorists," adding that extreme conduct of so-called "terrorists" was an announcement to the world that they could not receive justice in ruling class courts or through mainstream channels. Calling his attention to a 27 June 1994 letter from Insurgent Subcommander Marcos of the Zapatista Army of National Liberation to the Mexican novelist, Carlos Fuentes, in Mexico City, I read the following excerpt:

> But I must do everything I can to convince you that, for weapons to fall silent, ideas must speak – and must speak loudly, more loudly than bullets. I must convince you not only that we cannot alone, carry this banner that ripples anew, with its indigenous blood, above our soil. I must also convince you that we do not want to carry it alone, that we want others, better and wiser than us, to raise it with us. I must convince you that the long night of ignominy that oppressed us all these decades...is not necessarily followed by a dawn, that the night might well be followed by another night if we do not, by force of reason, end it now.[13]

After reading the excerpt to him the phone fell silent. It seemed as though a minute had passed before we began to talk about Fuentes' response to what amounted to a stiff challenge from Subcommander Marcos. I outlined Fuentes' response for my friend. In essence, Fuentes believed that the Zapatistas response in Southern Mexico was wrong – an armed rebellion was unwarranted. My friend asked me what did I think about Fuentes' judgment.

I told him that Fuentes could neither hear nor understand what Insurgent Subcommander Marcos was saying. Perched on top of the world with all his advantages, he only knew the language of disengaged and insensitive winners and could only respond to Subcommander Marcos in terms inappropriate to those who had endured oppression. Being from above, i.e., not in the trenches of the campesinos, the leisure class Fuentes could only speak of justice and democracy as a person whose destiny was not determined by the uncertainties of the bush. He was an intellectual academic, who dealt in discourse but not in experience. He could not imagine the slow death of the disallowed peasants of Chiapas. I indicated that Subcomander Marcos knew that process. His opposition to it made him the masked man of the wilderness, cast out as he was on the edge of existence. For Fuentes the justice that Subcommander Marcos and the Zapatistas sought could have been obtained as a bourgeois academic would envision.[14] But could they have gone about it in the way Fuentes suggested after pleading a cause that had mushroomed into desperation over a century?

My friend then questioned my credentials or expertise on the subject, urging me to stick to making comments on biblical subjects since I was neither an expert on terrorists, nor on Chiapas. Admitting my "non-expert" status to him, I went on to tell him that I could not be quiet while the world burned around me. I told him I was tired of being boxed in because of decisions others made for me, that sometimes the deep wells of life and resourcefulness are in obscure locations, and that real experts are not always on Main Street. I wagered that non-experts had solved more problems than experts, using as an example the biblical non-expert Daniel who solved a riddle that Babylonian experts never could. I offered that it might not be beyond experts in some instances to have a vested interest in continuing issues that average people could have solved long ago. "Experts do make a living out of being professional experts," I said. I asked him what would doctors do if everyone suddenly became well? I said to him: "I am no expert on terrorists and terrorism, but for years I had been concerned about it." Then I reminded my friend of a statement I once made in a Boston newspaper on terrorism long ago: "Terrorism is the last ditch effort on the part of the oppressed to get the attention of the oppressor."

While those words jarred my friend just as Marcos' words to Fuentes had, he was civil. He noted that we could pick up the conversation later. We closed abruptly.

Notes to Chapter One

1. *USA Today*, August 23, 1998, 6a.
2. *World Press Review*, November 1998, 45/11:10.
3. Ibid.
4. *The Charlotte Observer*, August 22, 1998, 14a.
5. Ibid.
6. Yossef Bodansky, *Bin Laden: The Man Who Declared War on America* (Rocklin, California: Prima Publishing, 1999).
7. Raymond Bonner and Steve LeVine. "'We Are Freedom Fighters,' Says a Leader of Militants." *The New York Times* (1998): n. pag. Online. Internet. 18 Sept. 1998. Available: *www.nyt.com*, (August 27, 1998).
8. Bodansky, *Bin Laden: The Man Who Declared War on America*, pp. 262-268.
9. John Womack, Jr., *Zapata and the Mexican Revolution* (New York: Random House, 1968), p. 18.
10. Ibid., pp. 39-66.
11. Jorge G. Castaneda, *The Mexican Shock: Its Meaning for the US* (New York: The New Press, 1995), p. 81.
12. Ibid., p. 85.
13. Carlos Fuentes, *A New Time for Mexico* (Berkeley and Los Angeles: University of California Press, 1997), p. 123.
14. Ibid., p. 124-127.

CHAPTER TWO

Bombings in Africa:
What Does It Mean?

Tanzania & Kenya — East Africa

How incredible the whole thing was! I could remember nothing like it before. It was reported that "terrorists" bombs had exploded in U.S. embassies in two black African nations killing more than 200 black people and injuring scores of others in the process. Had terrorists from the Middle East suddenly put black Africa on their hit list? If so, why? Did black Africa belong on such a list? Had terrorists aimed at the wrong target?

Such were my queries when the jarring news came that bombs had been detonated simultaneously in the East African nations of Kenya and Tanzania on the morning of 7 August 1998 and that Middle East "terrorists" had been charged with the attacks. Indeed, the news of these bombings was about as stunning to me as the news that a fellow Jew had assassinated Israel's Prime Minister Itzhak Rabin a few years earlier. "What Jew could do such a thing?," I mused.

It seemed senseless. In my mind the innocent had been slaughtered, and a tragedy of incomparable proportions had occurred. Innocent people were in the wrong place at the wrong time. However when the dust had settled and controllers of discourse had paused, and I was left to my own thought, I focused on a number of my own concerns. I was not so much fixated on what had happened as I was on why it had happened – concerns congealing around the why as follows:

- Were the bombings in Tanzania and in Kenya a message to continental African and diaspora African worlds?
- Were the bombings an appeal to continental and diaspora African people to move beyond silence, especially beyond their silence on justice for the oppressed and trampled of the world?
- Were the bombings an appeal to continental and diaspora Africans for self-definition in the post-Cold War period?
- Were the bombings an invitation from the oppressed to the oppressed to reach back for those who have yet to realize civil and human rights?
- Were the bombings a warning to continental and diaspora Africans about responsibilities?
- Were the bombings an invitation to continental and diaspora Africans to consider the meaning of power?
- Were the bombings a call to continental and diaspora Africans to pursue the liberated life?

It is these questions that will anchor our discussion in this chapter. The winds sweeping through African worlds for more than forty years which produced these questions and radically reconfigured the world of African politics, identity, and culture, lead to two programmatic issues for our discussion:

- Why did the "terrorists" choose U.S. targets in black nations when their pickings could have been other American embassies?

- Were the bombings intended for black Africans as well?

My search for answers to these queries begins with the responses of Western commentators.

In the Eyes of the West

Terry Scott and Richard Shultz, as noted in Chapter One, had much to say about the motivations of Middle East terrorists in contemporary times. Scott stresses that Middle East terrorists (and terrorists in general) have been motivated more by religion than by politics in the last ten years. He also argues that the increase and spread of terrorist activities within the period was caused by "failed states," that is, states festering with unrest because of problems generated by economic decline. Shultz argues that Middle East terrorism signifies an ideological difference from the West, especially among Islamic fundamentalists who view the West as evil, hopeless and opposed to the way of Allah.

As fodder for their views Scott and Shultz (and others like them), pointing to marked behavioral changes in terrorists of the last decade, say that "terrorists" in the 1990s were more unlikely to disclose their identity and purpose after committing acts of terrorism than those of the 1980s and earlier. In support of this thesis, they offer the examples of the 1996 bombing of Khobar Towers (where there have been no arrests) and the puzzle surrounding the 1998 bombings of the U.S. embassies in Tanzania and Kenya. In the latter example, a group calling itself the Islamic Front for the Liberation of the Holy Places claimed responsibility for the attacks. The Front stated that it had launched a nonstop *jihad* (holy war) against the U.S. with a specific goal in mind, i.e., to dislodge the U.S. from its "occupation of the holy places in the Arabian Peninsula where U.S. forces are close to the Al-Aqasa Mosque [in Jerusalem]."[1] The Front also announced its "absolute determination to chase the American forces and ... strike at American interest in all places until all its objectives are met."[2] However, Western pundits placed little stock in such grandiose announcements, since the Scott-Shultz thesis

fodder – ppl available, but little value

45

regarding the hesitancy of "terrorists" to disclose their identity in the last ten years conflicts with these claims.[3]

Perhaps more puzzling for these pundits (and for casual observers as well) is the terrorists decision to bomb the U.S. embassies in Tanzania and Kenya. More than 200 Kenyans and Tanzanians died in those bombings. Scores of others were injured. Had Islamists made the formerly colonized peoples of black Africa targets of their attack? Was black Africa now on their list? Why then were Kenya and Tanzania chosen as first strike forums against U.S. interests in black Africa?

Western pundits have, for the most part, been unequivocal in responding to the query of why Kenya and Tanzania were chosen. They propose that the terrorists' decision to target those particular embassies was determined by two factors. The first relates to the matter of distance. The pundits believe that the terrorists (i.e., Middle East terrorists) chose U.S. targets in those nations because the embassies were close to the terrorists' bases or command centers geographically. The second factor influencing their choice, according to our pundits, related to matters of security. Claiming that the U.S. embassies in Tanzania and Kenya were less protected than other U.S. embassies, these pundits push the point that these "cowards" penetrated the weakest link in the U.S. security system (and nearest to their bases) to carry out their benighted acts. Supporting this allegation was the report circulating in Kenya that the U.S. ambassador there had long complained of inadequate security at the embassy in Nairobi.

Nevertheless, these theories seem a bit weak. First, it is doubtful that terrorists' decisions to target a particular site are determined by issues of distance. The bombing of the World Trade Center in New York (1993) and it's destruction (2001) works against the distance theory, as well as arrests and charges against alleged terrorists on the U.S.-Canada border (December 1999). Second, the faulty security system theory seems faulty itself. If the phenomenon of suicide bombings and the bombers' determination to reach their targets are considered, then one is forced to question whether suicide-bombing missions are defined by security factors. My

question becomes an essential one if Americans and
concerned about terrorism intend to break new ground on
terrorists and their motivations, especially in determining why
terrorists strike some targets and not others. Indeed, if new
views are ever to emerge on the subject, Western scholars will
have to raise questions on terrorism that may not set well with
the public they serve. This chapter has a vested interest in
such views. It delves into the issue that Western commentators seem unwilling to explore: Why two East African countries were targeted by Middle East terrorists? Perhaps
nonconventional observers and respondents (nonexperts) can
clarify an issue that even now has not been resolved satisfactorily, at least in my view. Before we move into that arena of
inquiry, however, a few other comments are in order regarding the approach and attitude of our Western experts since
attitudes and dispositions toward subjects frequently determine what one asks, sees, hears, and receives as final render-
ings on the topic in question.

A Preamble to Other Views

Introductory

As noted above, Western pundits postulate that the terrorists'
decision to bomb the U.S. embassies in Tanzania and in
Kenya was provoked by the twin issues of distance and poor
security. Added to this view is the theory that the bombings
were simply an effort on the part of the terrorists to get even
with the United States vis-à-vis some undefined issue. I say
"undefined" because Western experts on terrorists hardly see
it as their job to inform the public in plain terms about the
real issues of those called "terrorists." Rather, they tend to
focus on U.S. interests, such as the number of Americans
injured or killed in a terrorist attack. If they do speak about
so-called "terrorists" their reports are likely to reflect U.S.
policy positions. To the government leaders, terrorists" are
lunatics, "terrorists" are inhuman, "terrorists" are indiscriminate killers, "terrorists" are fanatical, irresponsible individuals.... So their issues are no issues at all. In this vein Yossef
Bodansky, delineating events leading up to the blast in Kenya,
states the following:

...At first the terrorists tried to place the car bomb against the front wall of the embassy. They approached the embassy's front gate, claiming to be carrying sandwiches for the cafeteria. They were refused entry by the U.S. Marines on guard, and sent to the back entrance. The terrorists backed off without incident and drove around the building. The embassy's rear entrance is in a U-shaped enclosure with the Cooperative Bank and the Ufundi building. The terrorist tried to get past the gate and into the underground parking. The third terrorist got out of the pickup and argued with the embassy's local security guards, but they refused entry. With time running out – since the explosion was scheduled to take place concurrently with the one in Dar-es-salaam – the terrorists attempted a radical approach similar to the attack on the Egyptian Embassy in Islamabad in late 1996. The white car surged forward and a few terrorists jumped out, throwing at least one grenade and firing small arms at the embassy's unarmed guards. That action was taken to divert the guards' attention. Meanwhile the pickup truck's driver sat calmly about five minutes, contemplating and praying. Finally the pickup's driver fired a handgun and Owhali threw a stun grenade. The pickup truck tried to break its way into the embassy, but apparently the driver lost control for a fraction of a second. Nevertheless, right on time the bomb inside the pickup exploded. A couple of the terrorists, then firing on the Kenyan guards, were killed by the explosion. Since Owhali, who survived the explosion, does not remember if either he or the driver activated the bomb's fuses, it must have been activated by remote control. Most likely this was done by Fazil from the white command vehicle.[4]

The point, then, is this: Bodansky's description is derisive, governed by antiterrorist rhetoric. His description gives readers nary a word about the issues that drove the "terrorists" to instigate such a mission. How could it be otherwise when such views are tailored to bolster and cement Western determination against Middle East "terrorism?" It is a fact: U.S. governmental officials and U.S. media never cease telling the public that terrorists are less than human beings – indeed cold-blooded killers. So, as Bodansky's statement stands, non-questioning readers are assured more than ever that terrorists are not only crazy people; they are also mindless without a plan. As U.S. pundits tend to say, "terrorists" these days are unclear about why they do what they do.

Thus, the image one gets is as follows: The "terrorists" drove in the direction of the American embassy in Nairobi. Confused as to why they were there, they botched the job. As a result nearly 200 innocent Kenyan citizens perished, 5000 others were injured. Conclusion: Fanatics kill good people.

Are there, nonetheless, other ways of viewing the East African bombings? Is it possible in a world-house to hear those without the privilege of a public forum where they can present their side of issues that have marred and ruined their lives? Or should the privilege of public forum – one offering insight and direction – always remain with those whose rhetoric is often jaded? In other words: Is it possible to hear so-called "terrorists" and victims in a voice that Western experts seem unwilling to consider in this debate? Is it possible to view those bombings nonconventionally, i.e., as an expression of guilty by association, as graphic expressions of some vendetta against Tanzanians and Kenyans? Is it realistic to think that the terrorists chose those two nations for reasons other than the standard ones that our experts propose, i.e., that the terrorists were really after U.S. citizens but Kenyans and Tanzanians unfortunately got in their way? Should we permit our inquiry (given that so many Kenyans and Tanzanians were killed or injured in those bombings) to rest with expert truth, that the killers did not reach their target in time? Did the "killers" consider the risks beforehand or the large number of Kenyans or Tanzanians who would possibly go down since things can and do go wrong in operations of this kind? To reiterate – Is it possible the "terrorists" operated on the theory of guilt-by -association?

The above queries while non-Western in content and style (like the queries at the beginning of this chapter) are primal for asking pertinent (and different) questions of those bombings and for launching non-traditional dialogues on an issue that affects non-Europeans the most. Perhaps, these newer questions will call for an enlarged and more representative forum vis-à-vis terrorism.

In this arena of thought and hope the question concerning guilt-by-association will become definitive and programmatic for what follows in this chapter and, in some ways, for all that follows in this book. This question belongs, to be sure, to the category of the speculative and inferential as far as Western thought goes. It is an awkward question for Western thinkers since for them outcomes usually depend on facts, analysis of facts, and conclusions based on empirical evidence. The issue is not "what" but a "why." Furthermore, this query is likely to be beyond the boundaries of Western permissibility, because the Western approach (because of its disposition towards Africans and non-Westerners) is to declare unilaterally that it has the last if not the only word on world events. Because this has been true (even programmatic) for most Western history makers in the last 500 years, especially in the disrespect of Westerners for peoples with histories and traditions that differ, the tendency has been to think of questions of non-European peoples as questions not worth raising. Thus our "experts" get the answers they expect to the questions they ask. As far as they are concerned the bombings in East Africa were and are a U.S. issue, not an African one. In their minds the "terrorists" had a single aim: to kill Americans. So, in the aftermath of those bombings, the U.S behaved accordingly. Kenyans in Nairobi complained that U.S. officials examining the bombing scene showed little concern for their situation. They had to press the U.S. officials to note the magnitude of their sufferings.

So what does this mean for our question? It simply means that our defining one above is an African one. It is an important one precisely because it seeks to address an issue that requires more than Western intelligence to comprehend and to resolve. The point here is that the world demands more than Western opinions on issues that affect all of humanity. As to the issue of the bombings, the need – from a humanist perspective – is to hear from people who have lost much more, death and serious injury plus great moral suffering. So what do Africans make of these bombings and these facts? Is guilt-by-association applicable in this case? Before we explore that question in full, another takes priority: What did the "terrorists" say about those bombings?

In the Eyes of "Terrorists"

We begin with this line of inquiry because the views of Middle East "terrorists," like those of black Africans, are seldom heard in the West. There is an equally important reason to begin here: The perspective of terrorists, especially concerning the issue of guilt-by-association, resonates in a peculiar way with the African perspective on tragedy. Both go beyond the concern of what happened to *why*.

The point here is that focusing on the underlying meanings of events is not exclusively an African preoccupation, as I shall delineate below. Indeed, it was the foundation for my thesis in Chapter One, where I noted the difference in strategies and tactics between Middle East terrorists and America's KKK terrorists. If my thesis is tenable there, i.e., KKK terrorist activities are race-related while Middle East terrorist operations are issue-related, then the terrorist decision to bomb U.S. interests in Kenya and Tanzania is less arbitrary. In other words, the bombings in East Africa would have been issue-related rather than race-related. It would seem that the bombers chose Kenya and Tanzania for reasons beyond race, distance, and security since this is the first time that so-called nonaligned black African nations in post-colonial times had ever become a major pawn on the "terrorist" battlefield. It is a fact that black Africans and white Americans perished on

Kenyan and Tanzanian soil. It is a fact that no one from the "terrorist" network hastened to call the governments of Tanzania and Kenya to apologize for killing black Africans. It is a fact that Middle East terrorists claimed that they would target U.S. citizens and U.S. interests throughout the world. Were Tanzania, Kenya, and the U.S. one and the same in the eyes of the terrorists?

Thus the crucial issue becomes: If the "terrorists" perceived the relationship as such, *why* would they have such a "big bone" to pick with two African nations, especially considering the magnitude of cost to those two nations? Here again, Bodansky is helpful when quoting from reflections on Muslim positions offered in Abdul-Bari Atwan's article "American Harvest of Blood," published in *al-Quds al-Arabi:*

> The Nairobi and Dar-es-Salaam explosions are messages to the U.S. Administration *and to all regimes attached to it, enjoying its protection, and carrying out its designs.* They are a clear message written in clear letters and containing clear features. They contain numerous features: Either change the unjust and demeaning policies pursued against the Arabs or there will be more explosions....[5] (Emphasis mine)

Bodansky's quote from Atwan's text is longer, but the above extract is sufficient to show that the terrorists placed emphasis not on what had happened but on *why* it happened. The bombings sent a message, the terrorist method of speaking to their enemies. While it is a given that the U.S. Administration is *the* enemy in this case, groups that fall into the category of "all regimes attached to it, enjoying its protection, and carrying out its designs" might include Kenya and Tanzania. Certainly the terrorists, thinking of countries like Egypt and Israel, as U.S. allies, in this way may have operated on the theory that Kenya and Tanzania are allied with the U.S. against their cause. They might have viewed those African countries as friends of the U.S. and Israel, accomplices in strategies against Arab people and Arab interests. Viewed in that light, the terrorists were indeed sending a message to black nations as well.

But on what basis was such a message given?

Before the Bombings

In the late 1980s, most observers would agree that a radical change began to take place between the United States and Soviet Union. Ronald Wilson Reagan was nearing the end of his presidency and would not address the Soviet Union other than as the "Evil Empire." The use of this term was no more than an effort by the U.S. to debate in a world forum which of the two superpowers would gather the spoils in the future world, with Africa and much of the world, except for China and perhaps Japan, up for grabs.

For the U.S. the stakes were high in that war of propaganda, for the bottom line in the struggle, as well as that of the Soviet Union, was economic and political security in an unstable world. Access to world markets was a major issue for Eastern and Western countries in the 1980s, when national economies seemed headed for downsizing. Eastern Europe and the Soviet Union in particular stood on shaky economic grounds; and the economy of the U.S was reeling and rocking as well. Mexico and South America had virtually become basket cases.

To position itself to win the war of economic security, the U.S. in the late 1980s began to promote a policy of constructive engagement in South Africa. This was a chance for the U.S. to switch policy stations – from destructive engagement with 25 million Africans to constructive engagement – and thereby to gain credibility with freedom forces for future economic benefits. Consequently, by 1990 it became politically fashionable for the U.S. to dump South Africa's apartheid leadership and to side with Nelson Mandela and South Africa's anti-apartheid forces. With communist regimes cracking under the weight of economic turmoil in the late 80s, the U.S. and much of Western Europe publicly switched to supporting freedom forces elsewhere in the world as well.

The U.S., in particular, would return to South Africa and the rest of Africa in the 1990s under the *tour de force* of President George Bush's thousand points-of-light and one-world-order initiatives, human rights songs, investments, and democratic values. A sort of final volley in this trajectory was the African Growth and Opportunity Act, which the U.S. Congress passed in March of 1998. Later in the spring of that year, President Bill Clinton would become a mercenary for the African Growth and Opportunity Act in Africa via his tour of Ghana, Rwanda, Uganda, Senegal, Botswana, and South Africa. Earlier in Central and South America, the U.S. had staged a grand entrance, preaching the gospel of democratic values, investments and human rights through the North America Free Trade Association initiative (NAFTA). All this signified that for survival the world was becoming more and more dependent on U.S. resources and initiatives.

To ensure good results in the battle for Africa's soul as well as those worldwide, especially the soul of nonaligned nations, the U.S. constantly demonized Warsaw nations in the 1980s. As leader of the "free world," the U.S. touted itself as *the* guardian and defender of freedom, capitalism, and goodness the world over. Those desiring a better life were admonished to choose good health (i.e., the U.S.) over poor health (i.e., the USSR). In the war of propaganda the thinking was that any nation would prefer to be on the side of good in the great apocalyptic battle of Armageddon, where divine providence willed that good would prevail. To that end the Reagan administration prepared Americans for battle by campaigning for Star Wars or the Strategic Defense Initiative (SDI), the latter viewed as a preventive measure to save the U.S. from a sneak attack if the Evil Empire initiated the battle of battles. The return to space after the 1986 Challenger accident was another step the U.S. took to bolster itself if the battle came.

However the battle never materialized. By 1988 the Evil Empire began to erode, first in Poland, and then, by 1991, the Empire's overlord, the Soviet Union, collapsed. In the eyes of U.S. policymakers, the Empire fell because its economy lacked the punch and vision of free enterprise zones (free market economies) such as those of the U.S. and its allies. With no real economic competition left after the economic collapse of the Soviet Union and Eastern Europe – China being economically inconsequential in the West – what remained for the leader of the capitalist world (the U.S.) was essentially a mop-up operation.

Countries like Iraq, Cuba, Iran and Libya were the sticky crumbs of the Soviet fall, and they were targeted for the mop up operation. Their recalcitrance against U.S. intentions of total world control led to wars of sanctions against them, precisely because they had been unwilling to fall in line behind free market ideas that the U.S. and its allies preached.

However, what appeared more alarming and objectionable to U.S. economic plans in this period was the Islamic threat, which experts now say took on a new tenor in the 1990s. Strikingly, this new tenor became more noticeable at the very time the Evil Empire was collapsing and the Cold War was ending. In this period also the U.S. began to preach the gospel of a one-world order and the spread of a thousand points of light. The result was that the U.S. not only began to take over where the communists left off; it developed a policy to keep at bay the only existing threat to its expansion and its access to the resources of the Muslim world. It invaded that world in an impressive way in 1990 under the banner of freedom and democratic values, initially under the aegis of extricating Iraq from Kuwait, an action that mushroomed into posting U.S. troops in Saudi Arabia and the Persian Gulf for the long hall. Thus, for the past decade the U.S., Europe and their allies have been engaged in a nonstop effort to annihilate Iraq from the earth. In this equation nonaligned nations such as Kenya and Tanzania, which in previous decades looked to the East and to the West for subsistence, found themselves in the vulnerable position of having to depend on the U.S. alone for the aid they had received elsewhere prior to the 1990s. Thus these African nations unwittingly found themselves turning more and more to the U.S. for survival, their roads leading to the U.S. for assistance. Indeed, they became client states to the U.S. in the eyes of the world, especially in the eyes of fundamentalist Muslims who wage war against U.S. and Zionist interests in the Middle East today. Kenya, in particular, is viewed as a staging ground for Western interests in the Middle East, especially the interests of the U.S. and Israel.[6]

If the picture of the world as described here is tenable, then the bombings in Tanzania and Kenya were not arbitrary. They were directed at the U.S. and its allies, i.e., those regimes such as Kenya and Tanzania that benefit from a relationship with the U.S. but in that relationship unwittingly find themselves pitted against Arab and Muslim interests in the Middle East. As such, Middle East terrorists would view Tanzania and Kenya as co-conspirators with the U.S. and Israel in denying Palestinians and Arabs their rights. Thus, in the eyes of the bombers, Kenya and Tanzania are proponents of U.S. and Zionist intentions. Their politics makes them eligible for the terrorist web.

Thus oppressed freedom fighters – not terrorists – sent a message to the oppressed. Perhaps it read: Return to your freedom fighting charter, and side with those who have yet to win their freedom. Nevertheless, how would the bombings be seen through African lenses?

In the Eyes of Africa

The facts of the 7 August 1998 bombings are glaring for Africans. Two simultaneous bombings occurred in the East African nations of Kenya and Tanzania. Twelve or thirteen Africans perished in Tanzania; two hundred Africans in Kenya; more than 5000 Africans were injured. Beyond those numbers was the aftermath of enormous suffering provoking the question, How did Kenyans and Tanzanians view those bombings? Did they, like the terrorists, think of the bombings as a message? And if so, what was the message?

According to Bodansky, the bombers, or their supporters, as stated, noted that the explosions in Kenya and Tanzania were their way of sending a message to the U.S. administration "and all those regimes attached to it, enjoying its protection, and carrying out its designs.". However, the U.S.

perspective allowed for no such meanings. In the eyes of the U.S. government the bombs, whether they reached their target or not, were intended for the U.S. embassies and U.S. citizens alone, not for Africans or against African interests in any way. For the U.S., the 200 Africans who perished in Kenya and the 12 or 13 in Tanzania were innocent victims. They died at the hands of indiscriminate fanatics. As U.S. charge' d'affaires Michael Marine said in Nairobi on the first anniversary of the bombings, "Both our nations and both our people were innocent victims. They were victims of those whose real agenda is hatred and destruction."[7]

On that first anniversary of the bombings Kenya's president, Daniel arap Moi, saw the bombings in a very different light. He was not as definitive as the U.S. representative had been in declaring the innocence of the Kenyan nation vis-à-vis the Nairobi bombing. Nor was he quick to discuss the bombers in the same negative terms as the U.S. representative had. Rather, Moi's statement and ensuing questions, before an assembly of 7000 persons commemorating the Nairobi bombing, suggested that Kenyans had come face to face with a situation that stood at variance with national reasoning regarding innocence versus suffering. Moi's statement and ensuing questions suggested that it is problematic in African thinking to join innocence and suffering.

For Moi the tragedy was incomprehensible, since the majority of the victims, in his words, were persons "whose universe does not extend beyond Kenya's borders."[8] He, then, called on the bombers, the assembled audience, the Kenyan nation, and perhaps the entire world to account for the seemingly unaccountable with two short questions: "Why choose Kenya? What is Kenya guilty of?"[9]

Moi's second question regarding Kenya's guilt is a traditional African question in the time of tragedy. It is the question of sufferers who are dealing with not-yet-explained suffering; yet it is a question that should disarm both the victors and the vanquished. If the victors (winners) ask it seriously, they go beyond blaming victims and begin the process of facing up to their culpability for tragic circumstances. If the victims (oppressed) ask it seriously, they make a down payment on their liberation. Either way both risk exposure. For that reason the victors tend to ask it only at the point when they become the vanquished; the vanquished tend to ask it when it is the only question left to them. For the victims life is as far down and decimated as it can get in alleged innocence. Indeed, the question steadies existence until something better shows up, for it is the question of the biblical Job, the victim, who wanted an explanation for what no earthly creature was qualified to give. Why do the just suffer if they truly are just? Thus Moi's concerns, "Why choose Kenya? What is Kenya guilty of?"

Moi's statement and questions on the surface presume that the Nairobi bombing was a mistake, but in African traditional thinking nothing of that magnitude happens arbitrarily. As such, Moi's questions are already an African judgment: *Kenya is guilty.* The only unanswered question for Moi is: "What is Kenya guilty of?" Thus, Moi, like an African elder faced with an anomalous tragedy as president-leader of Kenya (his African village), poses his question to some invisible seer or diviner. He needs assistance from those who are adept in identifying reasons for tragedies. Here the pressing concern is, What caused such a baffling tragedy?

This question is one that only Kenyans could answer through the assistance of a diviner. Traditionally, it is not a question that seeks an answer beyond the context in which it is raised. Rather it seeks an answer within. In this case it is something that Kenyans themselves have done – not the U.S. or Israel – that brought them such great sufferings. In their traditional society, when the offending cause is fully identified, appropriate measures are taken to ensure the community's return to normality. If the community engages in the suggested purge, then it would become free and whole again.[10]

Thus the bombings in East Africa, according to traditional thinking, is judgment. They speak of a ruptured existence and, in the case of Kenya, rupture in an advanced state. The bombings are either a message from the Supreme Being (Ngai) or a message from offended ancestors. They signify the spirit world's displeasure with the status quo in contemporary Kenyan and Tanzanian societies. The sheer magnitude of the sufferings in Kenya speaks to Kenyans' need to identify what provoked the spirit world to such fury and, once discovered, to re-establish a spiritual ancestral connected-ness that would satisfy the offence. Traditionally, then, the bombers are not just bombers. They are not fanatics or haters of Kenyans and Tanzanians as Westerners would like to believe. Rather, they are agents of the spirit world, dispatched as messengers to register displeasure. Perhaps the message is that further violations of ancestral and primordial intentions will not be tolerated.

In this framework the carnage from the bombings suggests that both African nations are guilty of ancestral violations. Here the thinking is that bad things do not happen to good people. Bad things happen to bad people. Most often in African worlds bad things happen because communities drift away from constitutional principles and ancestral intentions. Repeated violations bring disaster. So what do Kenyans and Tanzanians say about the 1998 bombings?

The Nairobi bombing led the average Kenyan to the message of harambee. Many Kenyans believe that harambee (ancestral intentions) began to disappear about a decade ago. Harambee means the pulling together of all Kenyans; it means proper society, where there is peace, love and unity among all Kenyans. When society is so constituted it is anchored in the ways of the ancestors. However, Kenyans now believe that these concepts have been missing. Some say that their absence is due to the introduction of the multiparty system – the Kenya African National Union (KANU), the Democratic Party (DP), the Social Democratic Party (SDP), the National Democratic Party (NDP), etc. They believe that the multiparty system, an idea the U.S. forced on Kenya, has been divisive, causing Kenyans to split along party lines. Even more demoralizing, they say, is that political parties in Kenya have been associated with different tribes. Consequently, some believe political leaders sacrificed harambee – the ancestral vision of the nation - for personal advantages and monetary gains. They say foreign philosophies and strategies are guiding present-day Kenya. Traditionally, non-African ideas as guides are perceived as pejorative and as evil spirits that destroy the community. However, the bombing, Kenyans say, caused them to re-experience foundational concepts of harambee. It claimed lives from all parties and tribes. As such, the country, for the first time in years, was forced to connect with its ancestral roots by connecting with one another in great suffering.

The catastrophe also provided an opportunity for Kenyans to focus on their nation ailments. It caused them to see that their nation had lost its soul. National unity was lacking; their society had become aimless; and they realized how far they had veered from harambee. Kenyans began to talk about corruption in government and society and the inordinate influence of the U.S. on Kenyan national life. Either way, the bombings, through African eyes, are viewed as an ancestral judgment. They are a wake-up call to a nation failing ancestral expectations.

But were the bombings a message for Kenyans and Tanzanians alone, or were they a message for the larger African world? What do they say to African people in trouble and to African worlds in shambles across the globe? Let us be guided by the thesis that African sufferings are a message to African people about what has gone wrong in African worlds. The great sufferings of African people, particularly in the United States, are caused by an ancestral violation called integration – a disenfranchising process the designers knew would destroy the African traditions of self-reliance and independence and would deliver Africans to false notions of freedom (bondage in and to the white world). The great sufferings of African people on the continent of Africa are due to African neo-colonial behavior. In both contexts African themselves decided these courses, and in both contexts it shall be Africans alone who must decide future courses for the African world. The remainder of this book will seek to underline these facts in direct and in indirect ways and, in the end, sketch a vision, albeit imperfect, of a journey of a return to African ways of ancestral expectations in freedom – deliverance from white control.

Notes

1. Quoted by Bodansky, *Bin Laden: The Man Who Declared War on America*, p. 286.
2. Ibid., p. 286.
3. *BBC Focus on Africa*. (October- December 1998): 9/4:9.
4. See Bodansky, *Bin Laden*, p. 261.
5. Ibid., p. 269.
6. See Simba Kamunono, "Kenya: Moi's Crimes," *African Perspective* 27 (Feb. 1999), Issue 18: 2. Online. Internet. 22 Oct. 1999, Available: *www.africanperspective.com*.
6. "Anniversary of Embassy Bombings Marked in Africa, America," *CNN 7* (Aug. 1999), *CNN.com*. Online. Internet. 22 Oct. 1999. Available: *www.CNN.com*.
8. Ibid.
9. Ibid.
10. See Jomo Kenyatta, *Facing Mount Kenya* (New York: Vintage Books, 1965), pp. 250-253, for an insightful discussion regarding suffering and reasons for it in traditional Gikuyu thinking.

CHAPTER THREE

The Quest for a Primordial Construct

The 1954 U.S. Supreme Court decision in *Brown v. Board of Education*, Topeka, Kansas, reversed the 1896 court decision in *Plessy v. Ferguson*, a decision that fostered, among other things, a separate but unequal school policy – one for blacks and another for whites. Since 1954 the government has sought to correct the 1896 legislation by mandating relationships between whites and blacks that had never existed before in America. Segregation, the linchpin and enforcer of inequality between blacks and whites in America, was to be outlawed and replaced by government-backed desegregation and integration. Simply put, a new day was initiated in America. Whites and blacks were no longer to be separate and unequal but together and equal. America was to be a color-blind society. To paraphrase Martin Luther King, Jr., America would be a place where one was not judged by one's color but by the content of one's character.

A desegregated and integrated America was to be a Golden Age of justice and opportunity for blacks in America. Since segregation was outlawed and integration became the American way, blacks left their worlds in droves to seek its promises. These promises usually came in the form of opportunities outside of black communities, opportunities made available to blacks for the first time in nonsegregated contexts by whites. For most blacks this was truly the Golden Age, a dream come true – the opportunity of making a living sponsored by white folk.

Nevertheless, was this Golden Age a good one for Africans in America? This chapter, through the prism of my own experience, will focus on my own growing awareness for some thirty years now that integration was not and is not so golden for Africans in America. For our conversation my uneasiness grew out of my sense of *ruptured existence*, i.e., a life of a people without purpose and a sense of ownership, a life without a primordial or ancestral center, a life exposed to and diverted by racist plots and schemes. Here I chronicle my own personal way of holding the line on ruptured existence. My efforts can be described as a return to *the other side of the river* – the life before integration or what continental Africans call life before the white man came, or life before the village began its tragic trek towards self-destruction.

Yearning for the Other Side of the River

The first seeds of my yearning for something other than the integrated life in America (i.e., what I call a *primordial construct*) were planted in me in the 1970s. Before that time I had no real longing for the other side. Why? For one thing, I was far from any meaningful discourse regarding the issues of worlds outside of my own physical setting. I lived an agrarian life. I had little contact with towns. In my world there were no newspapers, no telephones, no electrical services, no television in our home, and no conversations about world events. I knew nothing about the other side of experience – Africa – and I was not aware that my side in segregation would be my other side later. Africans in America generally lived that way in my world – rural South Carolina. This was the way of my teenage years. I was isolated, insulated, and poor.

Even if I had been in the loop of conversation about issues of my other side – Africa, hardly would it have been a topic for me. It would have been unusual otherwise. For one thing we had been "coloreds" for more than a century then. Another is that Africa had been slowly erased through African experiences in slavery and segregation in America. We rarely thought of distant places such as that anyway. Survival was our greatest preoccupation. We prayed for rain in dry seasons to save our crops. We hoped for mild winters, because our houses were not built to protect us from bitter cold. We had learned to depend on nature.

I grew up in segregation, a system configured by whites in America after the Civil War to ensure that the lot of Africans in America would virtually remain what it had been in slavery. It was the system of "stay in your place." As a victim of that system, I went to segregated, apartheid-like schools, lived on the minimum, attended African churches, lived among African people, and learned African folk values and ways. I knew no other ways than those of African folk.

A cardinal principle of the African folkways was *communal sharing*. This principle was lauded, from the sharing of food to clothing, from collective projects to community crises. Life was one big communal effort from birth to death. Perhaps the meagerness of resources inspired this principle. After all, segregation and discrimination permitted little to our kind. Perhaps sharing was pivotal and programmatic, because it was an endemic feature of African culture. The latter I learned in time from textbooks and conversational exchanges on Africa and other issues. Either way, communal sharing was the gospel of my rural setting. African folk in that setting had not yet learned to sing solo or go solo. Group activities were still in vogue.

Segregation kept me homebound. Or was it the communal spirit that kept me so close to where I was born? In any case, I was nineteen years old before I had traveled more than forty miles from where I was born. As such there was a lag in my awareness and understanding of things outside of my world. Yet I managed to squeeze a plus out of what seemed like a minus. I paid attention to my surroundings. I learned to commune with nature. I saw meanings in everything. My reason for being in the world became clear to me and quite early. My sense of life as a spiritual engagement was hyphened. I became pantheistic; I learned to view the entire creation as divine.

Being shut off from the larger world and its opportunities, self-sufficiency became a communal goal. It was a goal forced on our African ancestors in the aftermath of slavery and by the personality of segregation. It became a religion for us, but integration would interrupt and disrupt it. It made us something else. It was like Europeans coming to the African world to take over in colonial terms. It was a Babylonian demise, a lessening of African cultural strength and African self-help initiatives in America. It brought one-way lanes from black to white worlds, not vice versa. It seemed like a re-emergence of slavery – but in mental terms this time.

In the world of segregation my father and mother thrived on the religion of nondependency on the white world for their survival. As subsistence farmers, they owned their own land, followed the drumbeat of their own souls, practiced and preached self-sufficiency, owned their home, and equated debt with sin and slavery. They demonstrated and taught that one could be proud of what one had; one did not have to keep up with others; and that we should be beholding to each other and God alone.

To mark their independent spirit my parents belonged to the tradition of 15 million acres of black-owned land in America by 1912 and to the orientation of Booker T. Washington's *Up from Slavery* (1901). Unlike bards since their times, they preferred land ownership to cash money. They taught that it was foolish not to own land and property and even more foolish for blacks to sell their land to whites in exchange for immediate gratification, such as cash to buy new cars or for the latest fashions. They preached that perishable goods had no lasting value.

In the ways delineated above, we were counseled in prudence. My father and mother counseled that we should never "bite off more than we could chew," and few were our worldly goods, to say the least. Even today my parents' values, though both are now deceased, have stayed with me. In their example I learned that there was something "other" to strive for and envelope in the world.

At the age of fifty my father died, leaving about $25 cash to my mother, to my seven brothers and sisters, and to me. He made up for our low cash flow in real property and other assets. He left more than seventy acres of land debt-free, livestock, and a great deal of self-esteem. He left a legacy: If one was just, worked hard on one's issues, and did not sacrifice one's integrity one could survive all that life served up. I suspect that was the reason our parents never allowed us to work in white folks fields or businesses for spending change once tasks were completed at home as was the habit of some blacks of our neighborhood. On rainy days in the winter we always had to "shuck" corn. On fair days we had to cut the ditch bank, cut wood, clear fields, and so on. Inadvertently, my parents were teaching that life required that we work on our own projects.

My father did not live to see the life of integration and integrated education in the U.S. He only knew the traditions of African independence in America – African independent schools and colleges, African teachers and principals, African businesses and African power, African farmers and African marketing, and an African religious tradition of unhindered space. He knew the prayer request of worshippers asking the Lord to come with the fan in one hand and the broom in the other to purge the community of all ungodliness every week at church services. For him this purging was a sort of freedom from all impediments to African wholeness and self-realization in the low land of sin and sorrow. His experience in worship was judgment and liberation all in one. Worship gave notice to all of what was lacking. It released the community to revel in the ways of redemption once the benediction was sounded. Celebrants went away saying "did not our heart burn within us while the man of God spoke to us along the way." My father died in July of 1969 – a little more than a year after the assassination of Martin Luther King, Jr.

Being Shaped Outside of Eden

At the time of my father's death, the African freedom movement in America had virtually been transformed into a human rights movement. That change signified that something had also changed in the African world in America. Not only had there been radical demographic and environmental shifts in African areas in the South. African people were thinking differently too. In the former Africans – especially those in the South – experienced fewer restrictions vis-à-vis their movement in general and in the white world in particular. In the latter, the protest and sit-ins demonstrations of the 1950s and 60s (especially where the demonstrators faced dogs, water hoses, arrest for entering "white-only" areas and domains, etc.) by the 1970s and 80s had given Africans in America depth in courage. Many went to court and paid enormous legal fees to become permanent fixtures in the white world. Others died for seeking the privilege. Thus, on a large scale, it was not long before Africans in America began to think that the white world was the only world.

However, this disposition signaled that Africans in America had not thought seriously about what affects their decision to go integration (and so to join the white world) would have on their own communities in the long run as I shall delineate below. Indeed, the first order of civil and human rights campaigners, it seems, was to count and mark victories along the path of full integration in the white world, never to inquire about what their campaigns were costing their communities. Yet even with the obvious becoming more obvious by 1969, I felt no compunction to shift my own thinking and style to African-centered consciousness as a few nationalists had in raising the issue of Black Power. Black-consciousness as Black Power was young and debatable then. I knew it meant resistance to integrationist strategies. Certainly it meant African awareness and African pride. Nevertheless, I was essentially unimpressed and untouched. I was still in Eden.

The full measure of the stirring of these new vistas would become clearer for me in Massachusetts. It was there that I found myself outside of the African world for the first time in my life. It was there that I began to see for the first time how harsh life could be outside of my own community. It was there that I came to know the prodigal son as being more than just a Bible story of long ago. It was there that I became interested in African and African diaspora studies as a formal discipline and as a way of quenching my prodigal thirst. It was there that I became highly conscious of the other I no longer enjoyed. Before, I knew next to nothing about Africa or African peoples in a technical and academic sense. I knew what we were doing and had been doing in America, but I had not given attention to scholarly discourse about it. I was innocent and idealistic. I was part and parcel of the flow. I had not learned angularity yet, but in time I would.

The year 1970 began my transformation to angularity. That year was my first full year of meeting whites on a daily and consistent basis. For the first time I was going to school with whites. For the first time I was learning what it meant to live in a world completely dominated by people other than African people. It was as if I had been thrust out of Eden. I was defending myself unnecessarily. I was an alien. I was being forced to see what I never saw.

That year (1970) began the process of staking out the boundaries of my studies in the New Testament and its world. In the shock of ruptured existence I increasingly focused on Africa. I was looking back and moving forward at the same time.

Reveling in My Dreams

My studies in the Bible world made me aware of Mediterranean life and culture from the fourth century before the time of Jesus to the fifth century after Jesus' death. I discovered that the biblical world was not just about ideas and beliefs but about political and religious movements in social contexts. I discovered that Africa was part of my subject in major ways. I learned about Egypt and Ethiopia – the most ancient of African civilizations – the Sudan, North Africa, East Africa, West Africa, South Africa, as well as the biblical worlds of the East and the West. I not only learned about Jews and their habits in pre-Christian and Christian times but I learned about the tactics of Jesus, the human, in the struggle for Jewish liberation in Palestine and about St. Augustine's stress on justice in his *City of God* and in his *Confessions*. I became keenly aware that Augustine lived in Roman-occupied Africa as well as Origen, Cyprian, and Tertullian. I discovered the fiercely independent, revolutionary Donatist Church of North Africa on my own and marveled at its ferocity to stay African in the face of Catholic Roman domination and Roman culture.

I researched and read incessantly. I read the story of Olaudah Equiano, the life of an African slave published circa 1793. What fascinated me most about his story was that for the first time I saw and could see in print in a late eighteenth century account what I had been studying about African life, customs, history, and traditions that had been passed down aurally from generation to generation. I now saw in literary form some of what our enslaved African ancestors brought to America in culture and religion by reading the actual testimony of an African fresh from the Africa continent. It drove me to search for what African religions were before those religions were so rudely interrupted and altered by middle passage and New World plantation experiences and by Christian and Muslim missionary forays in African communities.

I read and reread Equiano, surprised to find in his words that his religious tradition was in some ways close to that of Jews in the Hebrew Bible. I reasoned that African religions were as old or older than Jewish customs and that the religious traditions of Africans in America were much more than a response to slavery and oppression. I eventually concluded that what our African ancestors brought to America was "preconscious consciousness," a sort of sieve through which all else was filtered.

I would learn much about Egypt, Ethiopia, and the rest of Africa in my studies. In so doing my angle on biblical studies and its social issues was focused. I formed, in time, a working thesis for biblical studies that to date I find no reason to change: *The Bible contains the story of an oppressed people seeking freedom from oppressors and oppression. Their oppression at times came in the form of the tangibles of foreign people and the institutions and regulations the foreigners imposed on them. At other times it manifested itself in the more sinister forms of social and psychological dependency which was often institutionalized by the weights of alien philosophical and religious conditioning. Either way, their goal was freedom from those who dominated them.*

To become free of these restraints and conditions I found that it was not beyond the oppressed subjects of the Bible to launch bloody "terrorist" operations against their oppressors. I surmised that the Jewish Passover tradition in Exodus reflected a "terrorist" response to oppressive conditions. After that war I saw that the Bible spilled over in blood and gore, because certain persons believed that fighting for physical and spiritual liberation was divine, indeed a way of ridding their worlds of unacceptable or unrighteous domination which often entered their worlds as invading powers. It occurred to me that the God of the Old Testament not only sanctioned war; the God of that testament was its leading general.

My use of historical criticism made this view unavoidable, especially as viewed from the Old Testament historical material when compared to the New. The Maccabean revolt in the second century B.C.E. appeared as the latest expression of my thinking on the Old Testament side of my thesis.

Returning to the Other Side

With a vision shaped by a more reasoned approach to religion, at the end of my studies I went home, to South Carolina, in 1975. Now it was time to take a fresh look at the world I had known from childhood in view of what I had encountered and experienced after a few years away. I wanted to take another look at the stuff ordinary Africans had been putting on the graves of the deceased as long as I could remember. These were the medicine bottles, the eyeglasses, the cups, the saucers, the dishes, the vases, the heaps of stones, the peculiar configurations, the epitaphs, and so on. These had piled up over the decades since 1865. However, upon returning to my ancestral home I found that too much of what I saw on our ancestors' graves as a youngster had yielded to modernization. In graveyard terms, it was called "cleaning up" the graveyard. Practically all the materials had been carted away – perhaps to disassociate black people from the charge of "heathenish" ways and to make them appear as "born-again" Christians and civilized Americans. At any rate, I reasoned that the removal of those graveyard items showed that Africans in my rural community were guilty of a change in consciousness also. My own rural community was cutting its ties with its past. It was moving from African outsider to American insider, from African distinctiveness to the melting pot, and from a glaring difference vis-à-vis African traditions to assimilation.

To be successful my community had no compunction about erasing its past. Integration demanded it. However, there were some things that the graveyard cleaners could not completely erase. There were yet epitaphs on gravestones that still said what they always did – "Gone But Not Forgotten," "At Rest" – and some carvings that could not be changed – laurel leaves of victory and clasped hands. They all reminded me of what I read about the cultural life of the African village, about the relationship of those gone of the African world to those left behind, about the space between birth and death, and about what was valuable and enduring. Those bits and pieces of the primordial world still stood and spoke; but, sadly, too much had been swept away. Too much was missing.

The Need for Paradise

In my search for the missing dimensions of my experience I journeyed to the coastal region of South Carolina. I knew from graduate days that much there could satisfy my longing, especially for things of our African past. En route an amazing thing entered my world – the Oyotunji Village of Sheldon, South Carolina.

Oyotunji was a village of New World-practicing Yorubas. Its inhabitants were ex-Detroiters, ex-New Yorkers, and others. They had come to rural South Carolina to put in practice the African traditional religion and culture of West African Yorubas. They sought to institutionalize their efforts by practicing a traditional lifestyle. The members of the community not only sought to do what traditional Yorubas did in their continental African context (sacrifices and so on). They underscored the seriousness of their undertaking by learning the Yoruba language and customs. This was indeed magnificent, I thought – African people in America unashamedly embracing a traditional African way of life in the midst of a social setting where most were forgetting the past and were now on the verge of going integrationist mad. In my mind Oyotunji was a reserve of African customs in America. It was a stabilizing forum for African values and traditions. I was ecstatic.

Oyotunji brought to memory my reading of Melville J. Herskovits' *The Myth of the Negro Past*, which states that African culture survivals were more pronounced among "the Negroes of the Savannahs of southern Georgia" and "of the Gullah islands off the Carolina coast..." than any other place in the U.S.[1] What excited me was that the Oyotunji village was not only near these islands but that people of African descent were conscientiously making an effort to counter the effects of European culture on African civilization in America. Oyotunji spoke volumes to me. It was a statement on the alternative life – a few Africans in America who did not want to be integrated into America's mainstream.

However, outside of Oyotunji's gates was another village. The people of that village seemed just as African, but they had no such awe as I had for the villagers of Oyotunji or their village. In their village, a village in existence for centuries, I encountered an indifferent attitude. When I asked some villagers if they would be willing to leave their village to become members of Oyotunji, they answered that they did not and asked why should they. I countered with, "Why not?" Their reply was quick and stern: "What the Oyotunji group is try-ing to do we do already, except we don't have no African clothes like they do."

After a short stint with those villagers I concluded: Neither the Oyotunji Village nor Africa was a big deal for those out-siders. For them, to be African even in America was normal. Indeed, they were saying to me that people who kept remind-ing others and themselves that they were Africans or that they lived as Africans had become pretenders. For them African was a spirit, a way of life. It was natural.

Something further surfaced in my thinking as I listened in my mind's eye to the prodding of those outside-of-Oyotunji villagers. It is that prodigals are the ones who talk about home and desire to go home. For that reason perhaps Africa became a preoccupation for me in Massachusetts, an alien setting as far as I was concerned. There I had to deal with matters and live in a context far beyond familiar turf. I felt that I was liv-ing outside of Eden. My life was becoming ruptured exis-tence. I had begun to eat in restaurants owned and operated by whites while black people passed by with neither money nor food. I had stopped feeling guilty about eating without sharing my bread with them, something I would never have done in my African traditional world. I was losing sight of my true self. I desired Jerusalem rather than Babylon, but Babylon in fact was becoming my real world. What was I to do?

Thinking Africa

In 1980 I was more than ready to leave Babylon – America. I wanted to visit Africa, which had become in my mind the way out of what had disappeared in my own world. For me America in general and the African world in America in par-ticular had now become a biblical Tower of Babel. I looked to that tower for the promised liberation of the Civil Rights Movement of the 1950s and 60s, but by 1980 civil rights had turned into a struggle for survival and a Babel of black-on-black crime. The African situation in America reminded me more and more of a patient waiting for the doctor's final order to discontinue life support systems.

A case illustrating my point surfaced as never before one October day in 1974 in Boston, Massachusetts. I was talking to a black undergraduate about criteria she used for picking her friends. I wanted to know if race played any role in determining whom she did or did not allow access to the chambers of her most private self.

My question was prompted by two puzzling concerns. The first was the mixing of whites and blacks in the Boston area. Growing up in the South I found this shocking. Race in the South I knew had always determined who could and could not be my friends. The second concern was that the student had earlier invited me to become a member of a multiracial Christian Bible study group. I was also asked to attend Sunday worship with the group for the purpose of receiving Holy Spirit preaching, but I had never thought about executing my Christian duties in that way since I honestly did not believe that the Holy Spirit could be experienced in a hostile climate.

To my inquiry regarding friendship the student said that race was not a factor in choosing her friends. For her race was a superficial term created in the modern period, that is, since 1450 to divide humans. She vented that the only determinative for her friendship selections was whether she and her potential friends had things in common. She noted in no uncertain terms that a relationship with the Lord determined who did or did not become a friend of hers. In her mind race was passe.

Her response disturbed me for two reasons. First, I had always thought from my corner of the world that friendships were and had to be race-based in America. The conduct of whites towards blacks in the segregated South deemed that it could not be otherwise. African people in America, in my view, had no white friends. From generation to generation, from slavery to segregation to trial runs in integration white animus against Africans in America proved that genuine friendship had to be race-based. How could it be otherwise, I mused, when history chronicled a different story? For that reason I thought the young sister had let down her guard and would later regret it. Second, I was disturbed because I thought genuine friendship depended on trust and openness. It was never my experience to have known African people in America who were willing to risk full exposure to people who had enslaved their ancestors for centuries. Rather experience had long taught the two-souls wisdom approach of W.E.B. Dubois in maneuvering the chilly waters of racist America. Now, however, in the student's response to my race-based concern, it seemed that a century's-old race problem was now being recast as class differences between Africans in America. I was beginning to conclude that the windfalls of civil and human rights triumphs, particularly of those in the form of social and economic advances and advantages, had deeded an entrance into conceptions and expressions that I found hard to swallow.

I realized that the student I engaged was a Harvard undergraduate, not someone who felt compelled to get her basics in some African institution of higher education as I did. Indeed, the more I talked to her the clearer it became that she had little or no experience in the sore issues of African existence in America. She had not known segregation as I had. Euphoniously speaking, she had not known the restricted life on *the other side of the river*, life before the crossing over into a promise land of integration. My encounter with her shocked me and caused me to ask several questions:

- Was so-called progress outside the African world in America causing Africans in America to become disjointed from reality?
- Was progress in integration and its ways causing Africans to forget the past, especially the indignities white racism heaped on Africans in America?
- Had the warnings of ancestors through their experiences within the white world been ignored altogether?

Nevertheless, I would not be shocked for long. It was becoming clear to me that more and more sisters and brothers making "progress" in integration were joining white conservatives in their scorn for less fortunate ones of the African race. Some were even riding the waves of an education of an "us" and "them" attitude. [And solidifying this view was mental positioning that was in part shaped by circumstances that the world had practically moved from a production mode to service one in 1974, i.e., from factory workers to computer wizards and from manual laborers to technology organizers.] Indeed, two classes would become more and more visible in the African world in America. One became talking-experts on the other. It pontificated on a host of subjects – the middle class and the poor, those who had and those who had not, conservative and liberal politics, American and anti-American ways – yet little or no action was taken by this group on behalf of their poorer (and often abused) brothers and sisters. Insider trading for personal success would rule its sensitivities. The other (the dispossessed) would take the road of drifters, as those despised and underprivileged. It would have no voice in the American world, except through the medium of lyrical rebellion. Either way, America's old worry regarding its race problem gave way to a class problem in the African world – the tendency of Africans to pit themselves one against the other in a context wherein race still mattered.

This divide, as my studies would show, was also prevalent among oppressed Jews in biblical and nonbiblical times. It was equivalent to the gulf that separated the Hellenistic unprincipled and corrupt from those Jews who remembered the principles of ancestral expectations and the charters of their liberation. Even there I saw that the unprincipled among Jews were viewed as the cream of the crop. In my judgment Africans in America were solidly on that path too, thanks to integration and its strategies.

Slowly converting from race-based to class-based preoccupations in integration, African communities in America would not grow stronger; they grew weaker. Integration initiated an era of African disintegration, for example, an increase in black-on-black crime, a 60-70 percent divorce rate, joblessness, welfare, new diseases, and a festering homeless problem by the 1980s. In this crisis I would go off to Africa in search for something other than a Babylonian experience in African worlds in America. I literally felt like an exile even among my own people, for what was quite depressing for me is that Africans in America willed that their future would be what it was becoming. They made the decision to take the path of integration. Would things be different in Africa?

In the Paradise of My Dreams

On 8 April 1980 I arrived in Africa taking a flight from Boston, Massachusetts, via Athens, Greece, to Cairo, Egypt. My trip would come to an end in late May, taking me to seven African nations. From Egypt (my first stop) I would go to Nairobi, Kenya; to Addis Ababa, Ethiopia; to Dar Es Salem, Tanzania; to Lusaka, Zambia; to Douala, Cameroon; and finally to Nigeria. In the latter I stayed longer, because I had studied the traditions of the Yoruba and wanted to spend time at the center and genesis of the Yoruba world, Ile Ife, but conditions and uncertainties did not permit me to go there.

Arriving in Egypt, a new sort of energy and confirmation stirred in the deepest recesses of by being. At last I was now on the soil of the oldest civilization in the world, an African nation mercilessly manipulated by subversion techniques and colonization schemes from the Persian period of ancient times to English colonialism in the nineteenth and twentieth centuries. I had read in ancient sources that this manipulated nation was a black one. I wanted to see whether that was true.

Egyptian blackness I had learned from reading the Greek historian Herodotus.[2] The African writer in America Frank M. Snowden Jr. had not only confirmed this for me in his *Blacks in Antiquity: Ethiopians in the Greco-Roman Experience* but offered much more on blacks in the ancient world.[3] However, I was highly aware that Egypt had not continued to be a black civilization. In fact, in the post-Christopher Columbus period Egyptians became a Caucasian race, but now in Egypt the tombs, pictures and artifacts were telling me that Herodotus was right. I was no longer a stay-at-home scholar reading racist fabrications of the "respected." I was now seeing for myself ancient Egypt close-up in the Cairo

Museum and other places. I was beginning to absorb why some say Napoleon Bonaparte, military leader and emperor of France, on his coming to Egypt was so anxious to erase vestiges of a black presence there. Perhaps it was his and Europe's need to rewrite the record to read "white supremacy." If so, they wanted to put Caucasian peoples on the top step of the human chain of civilization. I mused that this was their way of making the business of African enslavement a more pleasant undertaking. I surmised that for them blacks had to be disassociated from anything marvelous in history and civilization for slavery to work. To that end some say that French gunners amputated the nose of the Sphinx for history's sake. But the lips of the Sphinx spoke about African civilization.

Being in Egypt drove me to reflect on how the interior of Africa became a hunting ground for European explorers and missionaries in the nineteenth century. I remembered that even God had to be a white person and that in the construction of the Great Pyramid at Geza Egyptian advances in mathematics, science, astronomy, religion, and so on had to be the work of white people. I remembered the efforts of European scientists such as Carolus Linnaeus, Johann Friedrich Blumenbach, and Peter Camper, who prepared the way for white supremacy with their chain of humanity theorizing. These scientists placed Europeans at the top of the human ladder of civilization; but Africans were placed at the bottom.[4] And at the bottom the only hope for Africans was to become as white as they could. In that regard I remembered that in the nineteenth century Phyllis Wheatley received no credit for her own innate abilities to write poems. Indeed, the thinking then was that no black person could have ever contributed anything to literature or civilization without assistance from white people. In Egypt that view was crumbling before my very eyes. Then I saw the anomaly of anomalies: The conqueror of the world, Alexander the Great, had been brought down to Egyptian size in the Karnak temples of Old Thebes (now Luxor). He was Egyptianized. A European that looked so European in Europe had become an African pharaoh.

A renewed energy (because of what I was missing in America) came to full force one afternoon on the Nile River as I was leaving Karnak by ferry for the Valley of the Kings. En route a white male from America insulted me. He tauntingly wanted to know why I had come to Egypt, and alone. I told him in all seriousness that I had come to visit *my people*. Belligerently, he assured me that I was speaking out of terms, that the Egyptians were not Africans but Semitic and Middle Eastern people, and that I should take "that garbage" right back to America. Since I was reading a book on the Valley of the Kings he became even more bellicose in his instructions. He told me that I knew nothing about Egypt. "You are no Egyptologist, brother," he declared. I was now totally incensed but decided to offer no counter argument to what I thought was offensive and racist. In the meantime the captain of the ferry and the crew were observing his bazaar behavior and perhaps trying to figure out which way the windstorm he had created would blow. Before long I offered what was tantamount to a death threat. I stated that if he did not shut his month, in fact if he had uttered anything further regarding why I had come to Egypt, I would throw him off the boat and drown him in the Nile. The Egyptians were extremely amused by my antics and tough talk. Things quieted down thereafter. Upon disembarking on the Western side of the Nile the Egyptians praised me for my boldness.

Back in Cairo my adrenaline in blackness and affinity for our brotherly relations and bond in oppression would grow deeper and stronger. I was invited into Egyptian homes. I engaged in conversations with my hosts about Muhammad Ali and the black situation in America; I called at the home of David Dubois, the son of W.E.B. Dubois; and I found that the Egyptian knack for sharing was similar to what I had known to be traditional in Africa. Suddenly it dawned on me that I belonged to an enormous African world of achievement and flare. My relatives were everywhere. I met a family from the Arabian Peninsula that was darker in color than any of my mother's people. And in no place in Africa or elsewhere have I ever seen people darker than my mother's people. They are what we say of persons when they are darkest, "blue black."

I was now off to Kenya, my second stop, and would lodge at the International Hotel across from the tomb of Kenya's first president in freedom, Jomo Kenyatta. There I would become more involved with the people since, unlike Egypt, most spoke English.

In Kenya I experienced funerary rituals I had known from my childhood years in South Carolina. At the funeral of a Gikuyu woman who had been killed in an automobile accident, it seemed as if all the Gikuyus of Kenya showed up for the interment ceremony. When her body was lowered into the grave, several men with shovels began to cover the casket. As they tired others replaced them. I joined one of the shifts – a typical occurrence for able males before professional funeral services came into existence during my childhood – and all eyes were on me. Some of the curious asked my Gikuyu friend who I was and from whence I had come. He answered that I came from America and was "the great grandson of one of our people who had gone away as slaves to America long ago" and "had come to visit us." There was great rejoicing. It was in such expressions and experiences that I began to feel that I belonged somewhere in the world. Africa was beginning to feel like my home (and indeed my sweet home) as compared to the disintegrating African world I left behind in America.

I arrived in Zambia in the highest of spirit, but it was there that I became aware of Africa's problems. Though Zambia seemed more developed than Ethiopia or Tanzania, I just could not fathom why people were standing in long lines for bread when farming land was so plentiful. Then an emergency was declared in Lusaka – a plot to overthrow President Kenneth Kaunda was uncovered.

In Zambia I found something else more bothersome – Southern Baptist missionaries and their attitudes. It all came to the surface when I spoke at an opening convocation service for their seminary in Lusaka. I spoke on the spies from the Old Testament book of Numbers, chapters 13 and 14, stressing acceptance of the truth that tasks ahead are difficult, but that Africans can take charges of all issues in the African world. I noted that the report of the spies recognized that tremendous obstacles awaited those who sought possession of Canaan, but the barriers were not insurmountable if the desire to succeed resided deep in the crevices of our desiring life. I stressed that people of African descent were duty-bound to take charge of their situations and religion the world over and root out all that inveighed against their fullness in God. That was a major emphasis and truth of the text for me, but the white missionaries did not want their students to hear that from me. In fact those Southern Baptists wanted no advice from an African in America about continental African self-initiatives and liberation. They did not want to hear from me that they were not contributing to African empowerment. They did not want to hear a sermon reflecting the fact that Southern Baptists had been in Zambia for a long time, but had managed not to succeed in preparing one Zambian at the time to administer the affairs of the seminary in Lusaka. Nor had they qualified any Zambian to serve other than in a servant role in other spheres of Southern Baptist work there. The students at the seminary realized that. They liked what I had to say; begged me to stay with them for the term; and wanted to know why they had not met their African sisters and brothers from America before. I had the distinct impression that they had never seen an African from America before me. They kept commenting that I still had the "African hair" after so many centuries in America. Then I was a marked man in Zambia. *The Southern Baptist missionaries would not let me out of their sight both among their seminarians and Zambian church members for the rest of the time I stayed there.* I was spreading the wrong gospel. I was preaching liberation and restoration in Africa.

Fresh from the distractions of Zambia I entered Nigeria via Cameroon (Douala), remembering the issues that the seminarians had raised with me. They asked if I would send clothes or perhaps some funds to help with efforts being made in their churches. Those two issues, however, given the discomfort I was feeling because of those missionaries, never registered as something I could seriously entertain. At first I thought that sending money would be a real option if my sisters and brothers could focus on and define for themselves what an indigenous understanding or approach to missions would look like in Africa. But how could they, I thought, when white Southern Baptists guarded their every move and made sure that any efforts in the direction of African liberation and salvation would never get off the ground. I was totally against sending clothes because the only clothing I had in America was what I had gotten from European venders and designers. Thanks to integration, Africans in America hardly made clothes anymore. Therefore, I did not wish to contribute to African delinquency by encouraging Africans to desire Euro-American goods, styles and products over their own. Anyway, too much of this was going on in the U.S. I wanted no part in the promotion of Christian commerce and European civilization in Africa. I wanted Africans the world over liberated from such schemes.

In Nigeria I would connect with Yorubas in a very personal way. A teacher of mine from graduate school days had returned there and was teaching in the history department at the University of Ibadan. However, except for my former professor and others at the department of religion at Ibadan, Nigeria presented me with my greatest challenge. Not only did I find Nigerians a bit too arrogant; I had to struggle to keep myself clear of people who had nefarious intentions for my personal welfare. Notwithstanding, I returned to America from Africa on a spiritual high. I could now say that I, too, had something to say about Africa aside from the books I had read or from lectures I had heard. I was now in a position to make a judgement on what others had written or said. I could say I had seen some of my ancestral home. I was renewed in spirit and body. My diary 6 June 1980 gives a most passionate and biblical-like statement having experienced Africa for the first time:

> It is my hope to return to Mother Africa again, the
> land of our ancestors. May God bless the spirits of

> our mothers and fathers who were slaves in America
> for 245 years counting from 1620 and who were
> legally segregated and discriminated against for
> nearly 100 years. In the hundredth and seventeenth
> year since emancipation I visited the land of our
> ancestors. The record thereof is contained in this
> diary.

In time my spiritual high for Africa would wane. I would
come to see that I was riding the waves of a hope without
solid foundation. Nonetheless, it was the wave of that season
and the one I needed most. Africa was the adhesive I needed
to tide me over in an African experience of disintegration in
America. Neither the shanties I saw on my way from the air-
port to downtown Douala nor the begging poor of the streets
in Ethiopia jarred my spiritual high in 1980. I was drunk in
nonrealism. The rumblings of Zambia should have awakened
me, but they did not. The end of the great dream of Kwame
Nkrumah regarding a unified Africa should have said that
Africa was less than I thought, but in 1980 I needed a mindset that was different from America. The rumors that sisters
and brothers on the continent were involved to some extent
in the nasty business of the slave trade should have jolted me
in 1980, but I had no use for negatives about Mother Africa
then. Then I had only learned to hear that the miseries of
Ethiopia and the rest of Africa were to be blamed on others,
never on Africans themselves. That view was nonancestral, yet
I chose to be guided by it. And this was my situation despite
all I had gathered from traditional African religions and
philosophies regarding the placement of blame.

My thinking was not significantly altered when it came to
the mess of African existence in America. I had only learned
to read of the behavior of the priest and the Levite in the
story of the Good Samaritan as conduct of ruthless white folks
whose indifference to black suffering caused them to pass a
battered black man in the ditch without a pause. Whites folks
in racist America are just like that was my line. I had not yet
arrived at the point where I could think of those two charac-

ters as continental and diaspora Africans vis-à-vis attitudes about the oppressed and abused. I was in no mood to change my mind on the global reality of the African problem. I just could not permit a hermeneutic perspective that would allow for unfavorable messages regarding my ancestral home. For me Africa had to be my paradise, the one primordial construct left in the world for Africans in the diaspora. It was innocent, indeed it had to be, because I needed an image far different from the disintegrating black situation in America. I was dreaming. I did not want to face up to the fact that good in Africa, if good had ever been there, had disintegrated. The reason became a preoccupation for me in time.

Notes

1. Melville J. Herskovits, *The Myth of the Negro Past* (1941; Reprint, Gloucester, Massachusetts: Peter Smith, 1970).
2. *Herodotus* I, 2:57.
3. Frank M. Snowden, Jr., *Blacks in Antiquities: Ethiopians in the Greco-Roman Experience* (Cambridge: The Belknap Press of Harvard University Press, 1970).
4. For an insightful discussion on this matter, see Winthrop D. Jordan, *White Over Black: American Attitudes Toward the Negro*, 1550-1812 (Chapel Hill, North Carolina: The University of North Carolina Press, 1968), pp. 216-252.

CHAPTER FOUR

Facing Up in Exile: African Reality in the United States

My preoccupation with Africa and my journey there was caused by my sense that the African world was disintegrating in America. It was my way of dealing with regret. I regretted that the culture of communal ways that had sustained Africans in America since slavery (and in the worst of times) was becoming a thing of the past. For me these ways were ancestral ways. They came to America with the Africans from the continent. I reasoned that they defeated slavery and steadied Africans in their sufferings throughout segregation but since the 1980s were becoming archival remembrances. What was more disturbing for me is that integrationist ways were supplanting them. The latter birthed individualism and brought pandemic chaos to African worlds.

This chapter will show how integration re-enslaved Africans in America. From exhibits of independence and solidarity in segregation, Africans became a workforce for others with few benefits, all in the name of freedom and progress as deemed by integration. This chapter will not only delineate ways I employed to register my resistance to integration and disintegration. It will demonstrate the depth of my deep concern that integration would return Africans in America to the bondage from which the freedom movement had released them.

Life under Integration

The road of integration was and is a one-way street in America – a movement of blacks from traditional Africa worlds to white worlds, but not the other way around. Persons of African descent under the plan comply with its demand when they leave historic African communities in America for work, membership, and rank in the white world. The presupposition here is that the white world has what the black world needs.

To become productive individuals under the terms of integration Africans in America relinquished control over major aspects of their affairs. In so many instances this meant severing ties with familiar connections – African families, communities, businesses, farms, workplaces, and so on – for a life and functions beyond them. The desired objective of its supporters was to live the American dream by feasting on opportunities the larger white world offered. As such freedom, defined as life free of white control by African ancestors in slavery and in Civil Rights Movement of the 1950s and 60s, was reconfigured by integrationist Africans to mean life chances in a white-controlled context. As a result African independence was redefined in the 1970s and 80s. It no longer meant getting away from white control as it had for Africans in slavery and segregation. Instead, it meant the opportunity to be controlled by white America. Thus, the freedom culture of the African world that had been ritualized and safeguarded in African communities and in African churches, in African homes and in other institutions for more than 100 years since slavery in America was terminated by Africans in America and sent into exile after the 1960s. Thereafter the white world became *the* world for most African people in

America. In a word, Africans took up residence at a new address in America – the one-way street of integration.

The African decision to take integration's road became plain in time; fewer African teachers would help to shape the minds of African students in public school settings, diminished ownership of land compared with preintegration times, lack of role models in the freedom tradition of Africa, unnecessary dependency on white America.... In schools, for example, white teachers took charge of classrooms filled with African students and instructed them. Directives regarding African values and on how to get from point A to point B, a function once the responsibility of African teachers and African administrators in the schools of preintegration days, became largely the responsibility of white teachers and white administrators. In too many instances African dreams became hostages of racist venting. This is because African students no longer had the models that kept them afloat when they were beyond the reach of their parents and homes, as it was in preintegration settings. They hardly benefited from those African teachers and administrators who managed to stay in the postintegration system. These, almost without exception, became second-class citizens in integration. Under integrationist rules they were forbidden to offer African pupils the special care and assistance they needed – forbidden as they were to focus on African concerns under the doctrine of equal opportunity for all. For them to do otherwise would have been a violation of the very thing integration on paper sought to prohibit – the equating of race with privileges.

Under such strictures, white racist teachers gained a strategic advantage over the African world: They made sure that African students would not reach their highest potential through career counseling advisement. For that reason integrated school settings were and are microcosmic zones of America's racial history and America's race problem.

While some educational institutions, especially those beyond the high school level, recognized the magnitude of this problem in the form of cultural awareness series, African and African-American studies, multicultural studies, etc., even here something was and is still missing. The fact is that in such efforts a kind of truth is espoused that favors European-America's heritage and tradition – not truth favorable to African people and their history in America and in other contexts. Thus, integration deemed that "truths" about Africans in America and elsewhere would be filtered through integrationist lenses for integrationist goals by scholars and researchers far from African settings and indifferent to African concerns. The objective is to construct a revisionist history to ensure that Africans in America would always be ardent supporters and missionaries of integrationist intentions. For that reason European-American institutions and agencies invest large sums to ensure that the African story is told from a European-American perspective, told by scholars approved by them and under the tutelage of their institutions. The psychology at work here is to produce an "official" portrait of African life and history that Euro-America can live with. African truth becomes what is good for America's future. The hope is that the story of the poor African woman who gave Booker T. Washington six eggs to assist in the building up of the African world at Tuskegee would be forgotten and replaced by African stories showing Africans building up the white world.[1]

In these ways and others the creative techniques and strategies Africans developed for survival and wellbeing in America were disassembled under integration. African energy and ingenuity were conscripted and enlisted for projects in which Africans had neither voice nor vote. Such worlds produced the likes of Magic Johnson and Michael Jordan who became money-making machines for white owners and white sponsors in the sports world. As sports figures their responsibility was to lure African youngsters (often poor) into a false sense of prestige and power through sportswear bearing their names in bold letters while hiding the names of their sponsors in smaller print. Nevertheless poor African youngsters suffered in the process. The little money they had was siphoned off and interred in the coffers of owners and producers by means of a strange psychology: The youngsters wearing the sportswear became instant superheroes. They became Magic and Mike without resources.

Thus, Carter G. Woodson's chastisement regarding indiscriminate use of African resources went unheeded.[2] Indeed, a heavier load than necessary became the lot of those who needed no additional responsibilities in an already over-taxed system.

Ways of the Upwardly Mobile

Initially integration was not a white initiative but a black one. At first whites saw no economic and social benefit in it. Blacks did. In hindsight it was an African bourgeois initiative that turned into national policy; yet no national referendum was ever offered that Africans could have voted it up or down. Instead, the African bourgeois leadership in America simply assumed that it was best for all and went about the business of negotiating its permanence and particulars. Thus, opposition in African communities expressed by nationalists and resistance in white communities by segregationists in the South and in the North went unrecognized as serious challenges. In fact, the bourgeois leadership spent enormous amounts of money, talent, and energy in court cases and life-threatening situations to ensure that integration would become the nation's creed. In hindsight that leadership seemed possessed by a single motivating idea: Whites have what blacks need. However, more was at stake. That leadership wanted the chance to prove to whites that their truth for centuries about African inferiority was simply untrue. Thus, integration was driven by a *blacks-are-not inferior philosophy, but that given a chance in the white world blacks could stand shoulder to shoulder with whites.* Methods to convey that message to whites ranged from forced entrées into white-owned restaurants to pursuit of top jobs in private industry.

However, this kind of politics, I deem, was not good for the African community in America as a whole. Once sanctioned by rule of law and touted in the public square as the right thing to do in America, integration not only caused able Africans to abandon less able ones for opportunities in white communities. It planted seeds that eventuated in the division of African worlds – the African middle-class with values and aspirations at variance with the African poor. Thus an undesired result accrued: Ethnic solidarity in slavery and segregation was stamped out. It was replaced by the class-conscious ways of integrationists.

The decision to integrate would produce other unexpected results in African worlds. It not only widened the divide separating the African poor from the middle class. The middle class viewed privileges in the white world as bragging rights. Sprawled across pages of many a newspaper and in other print media one often saw "firsts" headlines. Some African integrationists rejoiced that they had become "first blacks" to serve on previously all-white councils; "first blacks" to serve as vice presidents within white owned companies; "first blacks" to go to white schools; and so on. Other integrationists distanced themselves from African institutions, African values, and African causes. For example, the best of African students out of high school no longer went to black colleges and universities. They turned their sights to Harvard, Yale, and Stanford, and in those institutions many enveloped and cultivated attitudes and ways of Ivy League settings and converted others to Ivy League causes. Still others took to defending whites against charges of prejudice and racism at no cost, and most became alienated from their African culture and tradition, including African churches.

This drift into integration and its expectations amounted to self-imposed slavery for me. It created within me an exilic complex. I would live in America but really did not belong in America. In fact I began to look beyond America and its ways. More and more I wanted Africa for renewal and re-envisioning, which eventually was realized in 1995. In between I carried on a protracted struggle to keep my mind and integrity involved with critical reflections and proactive choices. I fought to keep faith with a past that I believed had much to offer to an African future with value, dignity, and duty when conversations and practices in African worlds in America were becoming disjointed from freedom's meanings and constructs in the ancestral mode.

On the critical side of the ledger I reasoned that African people in America had virtually become a blurry shape on the American landscape. In my view Africans were not only integrationist mad but were swiftly becoming one with the American way. Suddenly brothers were not brothers anymore, and sisters were not sisters. The enemy lived within my house. African perspectives and practices now bowed to capitalist replacements. Goodness was no longer good for goodness sake. Suddenly it became a commodity driven by the highest bidders. This accrued because African integrationists had quietly become agents of imperialist principles and aims. They had sided with the strong against their weak relatives. Far too many disowned them. Like white racists they viewed the economic state of their poor relatives as an expression of poor decision-making. Nonetheless I reasoned that it was those "poor relatives" or their poor foreparents and relatives who went to war against forces of white racism and oppression for privileges these integrationists now enjoyed. For me too many integrationist beneficiaries showed their appreciation for what their poor relatives had done in scorn and derision and, in many cases, siding with bell curve theoreticians too. Furthermore, I reasoned that these poor battlefield soldiers (often on welfare) or their fore-parents opened doors but seldom entered the doors themselves. It did not escape me that the belated interests of the middle class in the movement for rights developed around benefits the middle class was prepared to receive. That is, only those with money and educational preparation could enter the doors of human rights opportunities. It bothered me (and it still does) that those that should have benefited were like unwise maidens left outside in the cold of poverty and frustration while the nonpaying middle class entered doors the poor had opened without paying entrance fees. Ultimately, there would be no real opportunity for the warriors who now face urban rot and rural blight.

African integrationists, however, had a different story. They entered the front doors that their freedom fighting-brothers and sisters pried open; they gathered up the wind-fall by the armload from the pantries of white guilt, and they departed through secret back door exits to the suburbs. There they formed new communities and relations. They joined white associations and white churches, took up positions in buffer zones created to shield whites from the rancor of African ghetto lifestyles, turned themselves into experts on "those people," and became government advisors and engineers of public policy, deciding what's best for ghetto sufferers and the rural poor.

Eventually these buffer-zone individuals took to salving their guilt in big brother and big sister arrangements on weekends; but more often they spent their time receiving *the word of God* from the wellsprings of those who had enslaved their ancestors just a few years earlier. Then a new and strange religion became popular. Economic failure in life was viewed as God's disfavor or curse. Houses too large to live in, cars too expensive to drive, clothing too expensive for ordinary people to wear, and debts too big to pay became a sign of divine favor. Embracing a triumphant religion these integrationists took to naming it and claiming it. They psyched themselves into believing that their god did not see color (despite all the colors in creation that the Creator created). Justice for the poor and despised no longer moved them, because their new religion decreed that the poor deserved their lot.

Rather than underscoring victories accomplished in the trenches as divine signs, they made spiritual gifts, such as speaking in tongues and biblical interpretation meetings, prime evidence of divine duty and approval. Prayer meetings became forums for promoting intolerance against those who are different. Questions about racial justice, ethnic justice, ecological justice, women's rights, human rights, and economic justice issues were pushed aside in favor of individual achievement and salvation. Prophetic judgement texts from biblical traditions and the prophetic ways were criticized or set aside for a menu of never ending praise for benefits accrued through unjust means. Money gathering became divine activity. God became an American. In short, integration caused

African middle-class religionists to leave unchecked racism in its most rancorous forms. God would work out everything without human assistance.

Thus, a deadening silence came over this group and the African world America as a whole. Rock no boat, see nothing, hear nothing, and do nothing in the name of justice and African welfare became the African way. Sadly, in biblical parlance, a generation arose that did not know the culture and tradition of the people; nor did it know what had happened *on the other side of the river* – the preintegration period. This was all due to the fact that Africans in America were now being trained to be systems players and promoters. Their checks were being cut by the system they once detested. The African house in America was no longer beautiful.

Witnessing and Resisting in Babylon

Incensed by the devastating affects of this integrationist flood, I sought to anchor myself in proactive alternatives, expressing them in several ways. Each was my way of voting against what I perceived to be another form of slavery, except this form of slavery was self-generated by the willful movement of Africans away from the protection of their own communities and into glass cages of uncertainty in the white world. For me this was dangerous since others who had followed this path entered a hall of silence forever. I knew of the death of the dinosaur and of the Carolina parakeet. Indeed, the Smithsonian section on extinct birds had taught me much about endings. I had not only seen a good deal of extinction there but learned why certain species no longer existed.

How would I respond to the crisis of African existence as I now experienced it in the flood of integration and disintegration?

First, I began to drive and fly long distances from Boston, Massachusetts, to Richmond, Virginia, to teach African students in a black seminary after 1982. I reasoned that I had but one life to live and I had to spend it with the oppressed in the service of liberation. I incorporated the Hebrews writer's use of the Moses tradition in Hebrews 11:23-28 as a programmatic sieve through which my students and I would view theological studies and African churches in America. I reasoned, as Moses worked on the problems of his people vis-à-vis Egyptian slavery it was our duty also to work on African problems. I would say literally to my students that we are engaged in war against oppression and oppressors. Paraphrasing the Hebrews writer, I urged that as long as racism affected Africans in America we were 'to choose rather to share the ill-treatment of the people of God (African people) than to enjoy the fleeting pleasures of sin' (white society). I would insist that my students read the story of Tobit from the Old Testament Apocrypha. I stated that the book of Tobit (from the Apocrypha) did not relate just to feats of a faithful Jew long ago in captivity under enormous pressures to assimilate or copy the ways of those who had enslaved and oppressed him. Rather the way of the faithful Tobit, I advised, was instructive to us as we struggle to resist acculturation and safeguard our people as well. I literally stated that assimilation and acculturation to the ways of other cultures and peoples was an abomination in the sight of God. I would say over and over that "religion is culture and culture is religion and that bad religion is bad culture." I would stress the victorious culture keeping Daniel of the lion's den, the message of Shadrach, Mechach, and Abednego of the fiery furnace, and the way of the seven brothers and their mother of 2 Maccabees. All these I noted were freedom fighters; those in power would call them terrorists. I insisted that these traditions should be read and heard if we are to understand Jesus in his first-century Palestinian context and if we are to understand the New Testament. Not only did I insist on an enlarged Bible; I did not shy away from seeing Jesus in revolutionary ways.

In this way (and others) I was asking my students to declare war against African integrationists and integrationist schemes. They were to go to African pulpits and communities in America in the spirit of Judas Maccabeus and his company and fight for liberation from oppression as Judas and his group had against Jewish Hellenizers and Hellenistic Greek rulers and institutions in the second century B.C.E. Buffer-zone blacks, I counseled, should not be permitted to lead us into a new slavery without a fight. I advocated prophetic preaching in the churches since it would press us to return to constitutional things of ancestral worlds. I reasoned that prophetic vision was crucial. Without it, people of African descent would perish.

I would tell my students that forces against African existence in America mandated that we had to find out what God wanted from us quite early in life. How we arrived at that was a matter of divine urging I thought, but the world in which we found ourselves had a lot to do with what we viewed as our duty in life. To concretize my point, I would give the reason why I let down my own bucket in the black world and in a black theological institution when my preparation should have led me away from black experiences altogether. I simply stated that I needed to satisfy myself that what I did in life was not just to think and reflect on things long ago as was expected of a typical New Testament scholar. For that reason no white institutions could make me an offer I would accept. In that spirit I was following the pattern of ancestors George Washington Carver, Booker T. Washington, Fanny Lou Hamer, Benjamin E. Mays, Mary McCleod Bethune, continental African and non-African liberationist leaders, and my own father and mother. I wanted to stop African deterioration and destruction. I wanted to build up the black world, not the white world. I wanted to work for African interest as my father had insisted. I was carrying on that legacy. I knew that I had voice, vote, and enduring interest in African worlds.

A second way of registering concern about the disintegration of the African world in America via integrationist means came out in the car I drove for twenty years. I had driven a 1974 Toyota. At the end of its career with me you could literally drive it without looking through the windshield. The floorboard, with so many holes, became a windshield. It was not that I was financially unable to get a better car. Indeed, I was under constant pressure to up-date all the time – to get myself a BMW, a Volvo, something befitting someone who had graduated with a terminal degree in religion. My siblings claimed my car was evidence of my playing poor man. Little did my advisors and interpreters understand me. I operated on the principle that cars gave signals to people around you. For that reason I thought that the cars being suggested to me were inappropriate, especially in consideration of my poor sisters and brothers. I believed that if I had gotten one of those cars for myself I would have signaled to them that it was O.K. for Africans in America to contribute handsomely to a world they neither created nor owned. Africans in America and elsewhere as far as I knew did not manufacture cars. Since that was the case, I wanted to be a model, illustrating how to live in a racist world. I did not want to contribute unnecessarily to racist strategies and oppressive schemes. I had not only learned this from the self-sufficiency exhibits of my mother and father and many Africans in America during and before their times. I had seen the same revolutionary spirit in the life and carriage of the prophet, the Reverend Vernon Johns.

A third way of registering resistance to African disintegration was exhibited in the clothes I wore. I had learned the gospel of "clothes don't make a person" that my parents and grandparents taught me. In that spirit I came to teach my classes at the seminary in shoes I had worn for twenty-five years. I never wore a suit and when I did it was not the latest fashion. In fact, on the few special days I did wear a suit at the seminary, my students were not only surprised but some would ask what occasioned my odd attire. My wife (now deceased) often pleaded that I not embarrass her among her friends and associates by wearing things that no one wore anymore. Exasperated she was more times than I care to recall, but on one occasion our daughter came to my rescue and said: "Mommy, it will do you no good to keep arguing with daddy about his clothes, because that's the way people dress from South Carolina."

Of my daughter's assessment I am not totally in accord. The real reason behind my minimalist approach to clothing was grounded in politics spawn by the need to respond to a new African enslavement. I was carrying on an old habit from the other side of the river, i.e., people of African descent had for the most part made their own clothes in segregation, created jobs for themselves by so doing, and had demonstrated that clothing did not have that much value. Furthermore, I deemed it important that if I needed clothes I would hire black persons to make them for me. However such persons had become rare in black communities. Integration had deeded the extinction of black seamstresses. The future would see such persons hired out to the shops of others. Thus disturbed by integrationist trends, I contributed as little as I could to African oppression by buying as little clothing as possible.

My uneasiness with the way integration was destroying African-centered ways, and consciousness, caused me to come to one final resolve – to broaden the scope of my resistance. Looking around, I saw that it was not only the African world that was disappearing in America. I saw that the worlds of oppressed peoples across the world were under the sway of capitalistic, disintegrating objectives. Cognizant of the crisis, I did what I could to assist oppressed groups. I would read about the Palestinians and weep for Arafat and the plight of the Palestinian people. I pledged to myself never to set foot in Israel or spend money among occupying peoples until the oppressed and denied were released to a life of freedom in their own land. I would offer forums to discuss South African and Native American issues. I became a soldier for freedom on behalf of 25 million Black South Africans and raised funds towards that end. I requested membership in the African National Congress (ANC). I got arrested on behalf of South Africa's freedom fighters and political prisoners. I would share with Oliver Tambo and attend the funeral of Harry Temba Dwala (the lion) in 1995. I would commiserate with Native Americans and see nothing glorious in celebrating the 500th year of Columbus' coming to America in 1992. I would not celebrate Thanksgiving or the Fourth of July. I cheered the Zapatista rebels of Southern Mexico; I protested the U.S. war against Iraq; and I wept because most U.S. citizens saw nothing wrong with killing 125,000 Iraqis in the Desert Storm Operation of 1991. I would raise funds for Ethiopian famine victims and for flood victims of Honduras, agitate on behalf of the disallowed, assist sisters and brothers in need in Africa, and side with the downtrodden. I would find no joy in being around the so-called high and mighty, but I pulled for the oppressed. I was consumed with witnessing and resisting in Babylon.

However, I was loosing the battle. Another kind of reality was taking shape in the African world. I was being exiled. I could hardly find a friendly audience for my issues in the African world in America. I wondered aloud: Had Africans in America moved from outsider to insider status? Why was it that Africans in America were becoming a group that had little or no interest in the issues of the oppressed? It did seem to me that the African attitude had turned away from truth to God and to justice to fidelity to country and to flag. It seemed that Africans in America were becoming noncritical flag wavers, and what was becoming more evident (and disconcerting) is that I had little voice among my own people. But I kept up my pace. I kept up the resistance. I was on a mission to save African worlds from the destructive forces of integration.

A Provisional Judgement

My thinking now was that integration had made Africans in America fictive figures. Never was this clearer to me than in the city where Rosa Parks' quest for human dignity turned into a civil rights crusade. Ten years ago I joined protesters on behalf of individuals who claimed their rights were denied by white business institutions of that city, but to my chagrin almost no interest could be mustered among blacks on behalf of those individuals. At community meetings (traditionally called mass meetings), calling for redress never yielded more than twenty-five persons expressing concern.

That was not my greatest of disappointments however. It was the rude awakening that in the city of the birth of the Civil Rights Movement it was no longer whites who threatened my stance but blacks who had gotten a crumb or two from the table of integration. It was they who insisted that I come off the picket line. Upon urging that a certain action be taken against a white bank for allegedly hiring a white person ahead of an African applicant when the African applicant should have gotten the job, I was told that I should cool it for the most unprincipled of reasons: "The bank holds mortgages on the homes of several of us. The bank has been good to us. You really do not know the issues. You need to come off that picket line."

In such a deteriorating circumstance (and others like it in African worlds in America), I began to feel that integration robbed African people in America of their commitment to support and practice justice. More and more I felt like a lone ranger, like the prophet Elijah who hid in a cave because he felt no prophets were left in Israel except him and him alone. I gradually became fed up with America and with Africans in America. I felt that a people who once had clean hands and pure hearts had soiled both. I reasoned that integrationist opportunities had given Africans in America moral asthma. I felt that a not-guilty people had become most guilty. It bothered me that mainstream living opportunities could abort so much that was good in a people. It bothered me that money and positions could corrupt good beginnings. It bothered me that people of African descent had learned so quickly after freedom to spill the blood of innocent people too. It bothered me that positions in the white world could render Africans useless on justice issues. It bothered me that integration was causing Africans to behave like tenants who found themselves at the mercy of an antitenant landlord. It bothered me that forgiven people found it so hard to forgive others when the time came for them to return what had been given to them. It bothered me that the enslaved could be as unreasonable as those who had enslaved them.

It seemed as if the judgement of Babel's Tower covered the landscape in the forms of brother against brother, sister against sister, and mounting social crises. I reasoned: Are these signs of ancestral displeasure with the way things are in African

America? Has integration destroyed Africans spiritually, mentally, and morally? Are things any different at home? My journey to the continent would soon tell me.

Notes

1. Booker T. Washington, *Up from Slavery* (New York: Doubleday and Company, Inc, 1901), p. 93.
2. Carter G. Woodson, *The Mis-education of the Negro* (1933. Reprint; Trenton, New Jersey: African World Press, 1990).

CHAPTER FIVE

Facing Up at Home: Negotiating for a Future

After fifteen years I returned to Africa in search of what I was missing in America. My trek began where it had in 1980 – in Egypt, and from there I would go to Kenya, to South Africa, to Cote d'Ivoire, to Ghana, and finally to Senegal. My daughter shared the first three stops of the trip. Later, I would return to Ghana for a three-week field course with students in the winters of 1997 and 1998 and in the spring of 1999. After my 1998 field experience I visited South Africa. I envisioned taking my students there for field experience in 1999 but was advised to do so at a later date. Nelson Mandela was retiring from the presidency and South Africa's future seemed uncertain. I would return to Ghana once again in the winter of 2000 and in the spring of 2001.

Africa did not seem as hopeful after fifteen years. Things now seemed drab. My exuberance that Africa would be my panacea in culture and repose from the disintegrating world of Africans in America no longer seemed reasonable. Cairo looked blighted and broken. The pyramids at Geza had aged. The Karnak Temple complex at Luxor no longer had its gripping power. Nor did the "sacred waters" of the Nile River. In fact, sections of Cairo reminded me of the worst of America's metropolitan inner-city neighborhoods. There was poverty and more poverty. Begging had increased.

Nairobi fared no better. Compared to 1980 it seemed less Pan-African and revolutionary. No one seemed to remember that a little tidying up once in a while could make the city attractive. Thieves were in business and on the prowl. Unpaved roads were the order of the day. Nairobi was spent.

In South Africa I met the worst of human conditions imaginable. Sprawling squatter camps of black people dotted the landscape. Two large ones were tucked away from view just outside of beautiful Cape Town, the beneficiary of Cecil Rhodes' wealth and privileges. Durban, made famous by Mohandas Gandhi, was no better in a different way. White paternalism was oozing all over the place. On Saturdays that city reminded me of towns in the segregated south. Black people came to town to spend their hard-earned monies; and whites took it from them in a manner that suggested that it was theirs in the first place. Then there was this irony of whites trying to ensure their destiny in a postapartheid world. Having gotten everything possible out of the system, they had now turned to promoting integrationist strategies. It was shocking: A few whites were coaching 25 million plus black people on how to transition to a New South Africa. Eventually, the trials of 1995 would become reconciliation without restitution in 1999. It all seemed neocolonial and American to me.

Africa was a sad place in 1995. It was clear to me that continental Africans, despite freedom from colonial control, had gone the way of their integrationist cousins in America. Both had gained freedom from European control in the 1950s and 60s, yet both showed evidence of an all-consuming illness; masses of poor and dejected people doused with a few persons of means. It occurred to me that continental Africans owned and controlled little of their world. Foreigners did. Even more depressing was that able Africans in both contexts cared little for Africans who could not fend for themselves. There was too much of the Lazarus-Dives relationship in Africa and America.

I then reasoned that African communities, African issues, and African conditions on the continent were similar in kind to African concerns in America. In both settings the poor are getting poorer while the more able enjoyed careers in self-gratification. Communities once thought to be attractive had turned into squalid towns. People were dull and lifeless in both contexts. And death was on the prowl across the African world.

I wondered why African communities had drifted to this awful direction, across continents, since my visit to Africa in 1980. However, that concern would be no barrier to my objective in 1995: to refresh myself in primordial wells of culture and meaning on the African continent for the struggles I faced in America. I needed the power of ancestral ways to wage war against African disintegration and disenfranchisement in the U.S. There was no doubt in my mind that Africa, our ancestral home, had what it took to reverse these conditions. My thinking was that if Africans in America could be renewed in the culture of their Zion (Africa), we could be saved in Babylonian America. In my mind Mother Africa was the salvation of black people in terrible seasons.

To what wells would I go in Africa for salvation? Where would I go in times when ancestral bridges seemed less honored and respected? In this chapter I come face to face with a demystified Africa and end our journey toward ancestral destiny with one crucial question: At the beginning of a new century is there a way out for a decimated continent?

African in Africa

My daughter and I had high hopes for the sacred precincts of Geza, only to be disappointed. We went there to commune with the Sphinx, but our Egyptian brothers did not seem impressed by our contemplative gestures and expressions. Nor were they awed by the Great Pyramid at Geza or by the spiritual delight we felt upon entering the tomb of King Tutankhamon in the Valley of the Kings at Luxor.

It was disappointing. While we were experiencing a historic and spiritual high at the foot of the Great Pyramid and reflecting on Africa's accomplishments, our native brothers were busy disregarding our precious moments. We were talking about Africa; they were talking about coming to America.

The Nile River, awe-inspiring for us, held no romance for them. It contained no sacred mysteries and magical powers in their sight. It was a source of water, pure and simple – Egypt's life channel.

Facing that jolting fact began the process of my demystification with Africa that would eventually reduce Africa's sacred precincts and sites to the size of places I knew in the U.S. Perhaps what I had read from the ancients regarding Egypt was true at one time but not now. Then Egypt might have always been a myth. Perhaps what we have from ancient writers about Egypt's people, culture, and milieu is no more than the uncontrollable exuberance of first-time visitors like me. America must be like that for first-time visitors too, I reasoned, recalling lessons from other situations. For example, I never saw anyone driving a car like my first one until I bought it. Perhaps Egyptians knew more about the pyramids than I did. In any case, more of the same truth was yet to come.

My journey led me to a benchmark in African diaspora history in the West – Ghana. I had come to think of the place as the ancestral home of numerous Africans in America. I had been hyped by the movie *Sankofa*—a restricted script about the beginnings of slavery from Ghana's trading coast—and had looked forward to seeing one of the places where the ancestors had begun their voyage to the Western Hemisphere and to the United States.

Soon after arriving in Ghana I was off to Elmina and Cape Coast castles. There I would enter the dungeons of the departing and weeping. I would place an offering on the high altar of sacrifice in memory of the ancestors. I would move down corridors to rooms of no return. In those corridors I thought about what it must have been like for those African ancestors so long ago, to leave mothers and fathers, sisters and brothers for a land of no return. I thought about lyrics from African Spirituals in America – "I Want to See My Mother" and "I'm Going Home Some Day."

On the batteries of those castles I experienced the suffering and dying of the ancestors a million times. I stood there weeping with my great grandparents, William and Elsie Alston, who dated their birth to the year 1844. From there I took an imaginary journey to our cemetery in Sumter County, South Carolina, to tell them I was home at last. I now stood on ancestral ground – a ground on which they, too, might have stood.

On those grounds I thought about sufferings of diaspora African people in slavery; yet no native Fante at Elmina and Cape Coast had nary a tear for me. My melodramatics were no big thing for them. In fact the very ground on which enslaved ancestors departed for the exile had become a business venture. We created the place, I would say, and now we have to pay to enter the very business we created. I was incensed and thought: Perhaps there might be a tinge of truth to the rumor that had been circulating for many years; that is, continental Africans had been involved in the dirty business of the slave trade and profited from it.

These thoughts brought others to mind. I began to think about what I was really experiencing on ancestral turf. I mused that the rest of Africa was like Egypt too. The culture I had hoped to find was either in the museum, no longer in existence, or hidden from view. I could accept that what Henri Frankfort had stated in 1948 regarding the nature and character of ancient Egyptian religion no longer existed in contemporary Egypt.[1] However, I did expect to see some of what John S. Mbiti later described as Africa's religion and culture in his *African Religions and Philosophy*.[2] Finally, it dawned on me that I had not seen what I wanted to see fifteen years earlier in Nigeria. I wanted to see Ile Ife, the sacred Eden of Yorubas, but I never did. No one took my interest in visiting the place seriously.

Then it occurred to me to ask myself two important questions: (1) Do Africans on the continent care about traditional religion and history at all? (2) Do Africans on the continent care about primordial and salvific constructs, i.e., the life world and thought of the ancestors as hermeneutic guide (and even savior) in a world manipulated by a civilization and a culture not their own? I wondered if continental and diaspora Africans in America knew how to distinguish freedom from slavery?

These questions generated flashbacks to Kenya in 1980. There (in Nairobi) I had met black African worshippers who, upon entering a sanctuary for Christian worship, put on European neckties to meet dress code requirements of their oppressors to worship God in their own land. What was more appalling is that their white pastor-leader-teacher from America directed them to do it, preached a no-earthly-good sermon, and Kenyans accepted it. It seems they operated on the premise that native culture and tradition conflicted with their newly found Christian experience, and that to wear the clothing of Europeans was a sign of civilization and acceptance by God. When worship ended, my African brothers removed their ties, put them back on the tie rack provided, and left those sacred Christian grounds imbued with cultural requirements in conflict with ones that were naturally their own. By this ritual, I reasoned, they were being encouraged to drop what was truly African and to take up the programs of Eurocentric believing, being, thinking and doing. Certainly their iceberg behavior during worship suggested that.

However, it was in Ghana that I came face to face with what colonialism had really done in Africa. It de-Africanized Africa. Indeed, what I came to see and experience firsthand in Ghana did not exist for most Ghanaians, especially those who were Christians or considered themselves upwardly mobile. Once in a while I stumbled onto an "old heathenish" practice, such as an all-night vigil for the dead, but "progressive" Ghanaians dutifully informed me that the practice was backward. Embarrassed by it, they glowingly informed me that progress and development would soon retire such practices.

Ghanaians seemed unaware of contextual theology and art issues in postmodern times. In Ghana Jesus was more often depicted as a white person. Their embrace of a white Jesus in a black nation was glaring, and unsettling. When I asked for the reasoning behind the acceptance of a white Jesus, I was told time and again that Ghanaians did not see color as an issue as their cousins in America did. I would counter by noting that Ghanaian art carvings were decidedly African. This was a dilemma, yet I offered a way out. I mused that since religion tends to point to vistas beyond the human and familiar and white was a symbol for purity in some African cultures, perhaps Ghana's acceptance of a white European Jesus encapsulated the idea. What I mean is that by accepting a white Jesus in a black nation Ghanaians were only continuing the tradition of associating whiteness with purity, the sacred, and the other.

However, my allowance for such a conclusion on the matter was not its final resolve. I reasoned that in opting for a white Jesus Ghanaian Christians of that persuasion had made a nonindigenous idea a sacred other. The point is the whiteness of Jesus is not a white-like-white chalk in Ghana. For Ghanaians Jesus, almost without exception, is a white person. He is far from the traditional white for Ghana and what white represents for some African people. Thus, the worst was aloft in Ghana: When devotees gazed on the white Jesus they were signaling a shift from black to white dreams and from black to white projects. This carelessness ensured that Ghana would be a white-black nation in mind, with or without the physical presence of white people.

The white Jesus issue was a serious one for me. In my mind Ghanaian denials of color were a denial of Ghana's history, especially the presence of German missionaries in Ghana long ago (from the nineteenth century) and the role those missionaries played in Ghana's uneasiness with blackness and in the depreciation of its native culture and tradition. In fact German missionary religion aimed to make Ghanaians black Europeans and thereby guarantee Ghana's allegiance to Europe forever. In some instances the German plan was so effectively executed that Germany-ism as Christianity took on a life of its own in Ghana. As such it required no further assistance from Germans or other Europeans to keep it afloat; there was (and is) no need in Ghana for a German presence to make Ghanaians think and behave like Christian Germans. For that reason Ghanaian Christians, in general, did not like the idea that I sought to visit the traditional shrine at Larteh. When I did get around to visiting a traditional shrine I was told that some people loose their minds after such visits, but these same Christians encouraged me to attend Christian evangelistic services conducted by a white religious leader from America. It was ironic: these evangelists had come to Ghana to heal the sick and save the lost.

The script on religion in Ghana played again and again throughout the Africa of my travels. Black Africa had a white savior and an insatiable appetite to imbibe and install as much of Europe in Africa as possible. For that reason Africa could no longer be the vital source of African spirituality. Intentional divides installed by Europeans and maintained by their evangelized African converts overshadowed traditions of the past. What of the past that was not hidden or denied was usually found in museums, in libraries, at old forts, and in the heads of antiquated professors who made their living talking about customs and traditions that most continentals did not appreciate. In fact, unabashed devotees of Africa's customs and traditions were now in the diaspora – in New York, Boston, Philadelphia, Atlanta, New Orleans, the Oyotunji Village, Cuba, Brazil, Jamaica, and so on. The continent was in denial.

My concern, then, turned to what I could salvage in such a disappointing dilemma. What could I do to save myself from facing up to the fact that what I sought in Africa as salve for wounds caused by integration in America was either not there at all or that no one wanted to tell me where I could find it? I was disillusioned and admittedly disgusted.

At my lowest point I began to face up in Africa and in the African world at large. Like St. Augustine, the North African, in his *City of God*, I began facing up by putting a shine on disaster. I began to think seriously about the subject of religion and culture, particularly the question of who cares about those things. I thought about what initiated my Africa *odyssey* in the first place – the need for something other – and concluded that a preoccupation with ancestral times is generally the focus of exiles like me, not of those who stay at home. On the tablet of my mind I began to inscribe my thoughts: that the Jewish religion really began to flourish in the exile, and that the beauty of Zion could only be a concern for homesick exiles. Then I realized something even more profound and programmatic: *The religion of Israel that we find in the Bible was shaped and forged not by those who stayed at home, but by those who were enslaved and abused in the exile – in Egypt, Assyria, Babylon, and so on. It was they (the exiles) who knew liberation better, because one misses water only when the well dries up. So it was they who noticed that the city was no longer itself.*

Then I was sad and curious: What happened in Zion? Why it seemed that so many things could go awry in Africa without a cataclysmic response?

The Thinking of Basil Davidson

In a 1992 publication entitled *The Black Man's Burden – Africa and the Curse of the Nation-State*, the scholar Basil Davidson, who had written so extensively on African history and culture, came to assist me in my perplexities. He helped me to realize why Africa's indifference to its cultural past should not have been shocking to me. He carried me to the very place where the process of disenfranchising Africa began. He stated that continental Africans opted to become like European colonials after their liberation from Europeans in the 1950s and 60s. He asserted that postcolonial African leaders willfully decided to promote the culture, religious traditions, and governing principles of Africa's colonizers rather than precolonial African ways in postcolonial times.

This leadership – trained as it was in European and U.S. universities – had learned through European teachers and professors how to show contempt for African ways. This leadership was trained to think of African cultural practices as unsuitable for the modern world. For that reason Africa's postcolonial leaders did not seek out African models for governance in postcolonial times; instead they opted for systems of governance that were most like those of their colonial oppressors, the very systems that had enslaved them. Wanting to do as the Europeans did, postcolonial African leaders led Africa's masses in the propagation of the gospel of Africa's backwardness and in a preference for things European. As such Africa was alienated from an appreciation of its own customs and culture. Nothing good could come from Africa; only good could come from Europe or from non-African models. Davidson notes how de-Africanization operates:

> Learned scholarly foundations, great international banking agencies, a host of specialized institutes devoted to "aid for Africa," have all abounded in versions of the same nonsense: a successful nation-statism in Africa must dispense with, or better ignore, every experience of the past. Tradition in Africa must be seen as synonymous with stagnation. The ballast of past centuries must be jettisoned as containing nothing of value to the present.[3]

According to Davidson de-Africanizing tendencies began in Africa in the midnineteenth century. Interestingly enough, they began at a time when Britain abandoned the slave trade (1807) and took on abolitionist tendencies. Davidson points out that the latter was peculiarly manifested in Britain's policy of rescuing slaves from ships bound for the Americas after 1807. Recaptured slaves would be deposited on the West Coast of Africa in Sierra Leone. Coming as they did from various nations of Africa and speaking different languages, these "recaptives" (as they were called) developed a language (Creole) and culture apart from native residents. They lived apart from native African residents and preferred the civilization of their British rescuers. Such caused them to view native Africans as backward and uncivilized, a predisposition that made them keepers of the British way in the "wilds" of Africa and missionaries of European Christian civilization. It was they who longed for the day that Africa would become civilized, and through European values and education they worked tirelessly to convert their native sisters and brothers to Britain's way of thinking and behaving. These British Africans (so-called civilized Africans) eventually rejected most components of traditional life and became Europeanized in education and deed.[4]

The end result of these manipulations is that Africa was already ripe for neocolonial objectives in the 1950s and 60s. Africa's proclivity for things European put it in the unenviable position of being at the mercy of Europe. Africa disdained its own religions, cultures, and histories – using measures fashioned for European aspirations for Africa. In the end Africa became all that Carter G. Woodson had earlier referenced about the intent of European Methodists who promoted Christian conversion among slaves in the West Indies:

> They [Methodist missionaries] were forbidden to hold slaves but they were required to promote the moral and religious improvement of the slaves without interfering in the least degree, publicly or privately, with their civil condition. One who served for twenty years in the West Indies said: 'For half a century from the commencement of Methodism the slaves never expected freedom, and the missionaries never taught them to expect it; and when the agitation of later years unavoidably affected them more or less, as they learned chiefly through the violent speeches of their own masters and overseers what was going on in England; it was the missionary influence that moderated passions, kept them in the steady course of duty, and prevented them from sinning against God by offending against the laws of man. Whatever outbreaks or insurrections at any time occurred, no Methodist slave was ever proved guilty of incendiarism or rebellion for more than seventy years, from 1760 to 1833'.[5]

Hence the European strategy in Africa was to keep Africans in subjection to Europe, whether tactics for such came in the packages of foreign cultural imports or in strategies of de-Africanization. The end result was the same: Africa became alienated from its own culture and values.

The Hard but Positive Thinking of George B. N. Ayittey

George B. N. Ayittey, an indigenous Africa scholar, delineated the current dimensions of African diversion, especially how things have developed in the social and political arena within the last few years.[6] As with Davidson, Ayittey surmised that Africa's problems today are caused by the missteps of Africa's past leaders, especially those who took over from colonial rulers in the 1950s and 60s. These leaders, he believes, uncritically adopted European models of governance once Europeans no longer governed in Africa. The decision to move in that direction was forged from Africa's acceptance of the European view: that Africa is a dark, uncivilized continent, and that only Europe could save it. So, at the dawn of freedom in the 1950s and 60s, those Africans who knew Europe best (i.e., those who had lived in Europe and had been instructed in European pedagogy and methodology) were thought best equipped to carry on Europe's legacy in Africa. In Ayittey's view this class turned African worlds into arenas of abuse. The results, he argues, are continuous power struggles and murders, especially among the elite. Nevertheless, ordinary citizens suffer impoverishment and death at their hands. Ayittey states:

> The politics of exclusion has been the source of Africa's chronic political instability, civil strife, wars, and chaos. Where the ruling elites had the foresight and wisdom to agree to and implement real democratic reform and power sharing, they saved not only themselves but their countries as well: Examples include Benin, Malawi, Mali, and South Africa. But where benighted rulers and hard-liners

refused to share or relinquish power, those excluded had no choice but to seek to overthrow the system or to secede. Either course of action resulted in violence, carnage, and destruction, as evidenced by Burundi, Ethiopia, Liberia, Rwanda, Somalia, and Zaire.[7]

For Ayittey the final solution to Africa's situation is in Africa itself:

> It entails the modernization of an indigenous African political tradition – the village assembly. When a crisis erupted in an African village, the chief and his council of elders would summon *a village meeting* – similar to New England's town hall meetings. There, the issue would be debated by the people until a *consensus* was reached. Once a decision was made, everyone in the village, including the chief, would be required to abide by it (emphasis Ayittey's).[8]

Consequently, Ayittey offers ten rules to resolve Africa's chaos, all rooted in the indigenous idea that the people rather than leaders govern:

1. Never Forget Your Roots.
2. Seek Ye First the Economic Kingdom in the Private Sector.
3. Privatize the Universities.
4. Demand and Defend Freedom of Expression/Media.
5. Practice Intellectual Solidarity.
6. Demand National Conferences.
7. Disband the Military or Cut it in Half.
8. Practice Pan-Africanism.
9. Set Up a Rival OAU.
10. Selectively Repudiate Foreign Debt.[9]

The Pessimism of Keith B. Richburg

Ayittey's hopes for a bright African future receive a more negative reception in Keith B. Richburg's *Out of America: A Black Man Confronts Africa*.[10] Assigned by the *Washington Post* to cover Africa from 1991 to 1994, Richburg witnessed the horrors of the Hutus' slaughter of the Tutsi in Rwanda. He stated that by the time he completed his tour of duty, African corruption, cruelty, and slaughter had overwhelmed him. Concluding that Africa was hopeless, Richburg boldly declared that he was no *African* American but just an American.

Uppermost among experiences, which led him to this position, was the senseless carnage he saw from witnessing the Hutu-Tutsi war. He saw dead bodies floating down the Kagera River into Tanzania. That experience caused him to turn against Africa. As far as he was concerned Africa's future was not inviting:

> I tell you, if you'll let me describe it. Revulsion. Sorrow. Pity at the monumental waste of human life. They all come close, but don't really capture what I really feel. It's a sentiment that began nagging me soon after I first set foot in Africa in late 1991. And it's a gnawing feeling that kept coming back to me as the bodies kept piling up, as the insanity of Africa deepened. It's a feeling that I was really unable to express out loud until the end, as I was packing my bags to leave. It was a feeling that pained me to admit, a sentiment that, when uttered aloud, might come across as callous, self-obsessed, even racist."[11]

The net effect of Africa's conduct drove Richburg to say that African America's quest for salvation in Africa was a dream cancelled out by actual conditions on the ground:

> But while I know that "Afrocentrism" has become fashionable for many black Americans searching for

identity, I know it cannot work for me. I have been here. I have lived here, I have lived here and seen Africa in all its horror. I know now that I am a stranger here. I am an American, a black American, and I feel no connection to this strange and violent place.[12]

Thus, for Richburg, Africa today is a biblical Sodom and Gomorrah. Only a divine visitation via fire and brimstone could end its sordid life.

While Africa may not be as hopeless today, nonabating conflicts, wars, diseases, and poverty point in that direction. Perhaps the bombings in Tanzania and Kenya is Africa's wake-up call. Perhaps they are a message of warning to Africans the world over signifying ancestors displeasure with the way things are going in African worlds, particularly the unacceptability of extremities in barbarity and injustice. Perhaps Richburg has spoken prophetically about the moral climate of Africa. Perhaps he has made plainer than most that African tables have actually turned since freedom, and that the ruptured life has become normal in Africa today. But is Africa as hopeless as Richburg suggests? Does Africa have to remain where Richburg left it?

The Word from Kakum Forest

Near to Elmina and Cape Coast castles, places where the Portuguese and the English traded for slaves, is a rain forest called Kakum. In it I found much more than Richburg imagined. I found the ancestors' path. I found an African future.

Compared with the activities of the castles, Kakum Forest is another world. Indeed it is a beautiful site, the best place on earth, it seems; when I experienced it for the first time in 1997, it signified, for me African life before two ghastly ruptures. The first, beginning with the Portuguese in the fifteenth century, was caused by white men in their coming to Ghana and to other African places to do business for slaves and other commodities. The second was what Davidson, Ayittey, Richburg, and others point to as that which fuels Africa's current crises – the unwillingness of so many of Africa's elite rulers in the postcolonial period to be guided by principles of governance that are inherently a part of Africa's past. This crisis is foremost the story of how Africa struggled and obtained its freedom from white colonial rulers and aborted it in schemes of corruption, instability, poverty, and widespread suffering and death.

Kakum seemed beyond both horrors. However, in reality, it contains both. I say this because in the beauty of that most arresting forest is a not-so-obvious canopy that I would call hell on earth. One comes unexpectedly to it. Completely overwhelmed by the paradisiacal nature of the forest, a sort of heaven on earth, suddenly you are on a canopy consisting of one narrow strip of board serving as a bridge suspended over deepest dangers and uncertainties. You pass through six or seven stations before you are free from all that awaits you in the uncertainties of the thicket beneath – wild animals and who knows what.

On the first leg of that canopy I completely lost my head; in fact, I signaled my intent to quit. I wanted to turn around and go back to my primordial safe-haven – to the gate of entry – but the forest keeper who stood at the gate of entrance told me in no uncertain terms: *The gate of entry is closed. You must go forward. There are six junctures yet to go.* With that, there was just one option for me: Go on and complete the journey despite the hardships of the canopy. Otherwise I could choose a non-option—stand there, die, and rot.

I took my only available option and offer here three concluding points about facing up and moving forward in Africa in the worst of times.

The first point is a reassessment of my primordial unreasonableness regarding Mother Africa as dictated by the facts of Kakum and my personal experiences in Africa. The second point is that African people the world over will have to deal (and effectively so) with the hand life has dealt them whether the hand is a concoction made by others or a creation of their own making. Here the presumption is that all African wounds are self-inflicted. [This point will be more fully addressed in

Chapter Six, where I speak to those issues vis-à-vis the African saga of mismanaging freedom in America.] The third point concludes that if African people work diligently to solve their problems within the boundaries of reasonableness, success is possible.

In suggesting these points and what follows I go beyond Richburg. I am an optimist. I remind myself through Kakum, as a child of nature, that I was nurtured on the religion of optimism. I am used to seeing a dying sun of late afternoon return to the world in glowing vigor the next morning. Indeed, I heard all my life from ordinary black people in the worst of conditions on earth that brighter days were coming and dark clouds were passing away. I also heard these ordinary people talking about freedom when none was obvious. To my continental side these are the thoughts and expressions of my Joseph side and the actions of exiles and slaves. They tell of a dogged determination to see morning in the worst and longest of nights. Slaves and exiles are the messengers and the preservers of African indigenous traditions.

Thus, the first message from Kakum is that Africans cannot go back to where they have been in the past. Life on the move is unlike that. There is a closed-ness, a bar to yesterdays whether those yesterdays were good or bad. Yesterday can never be again. Kakum's door was closed behind me. The wisdom of the age and the keeper of the forest (the guard) instructed me to move ahead. Such instructions seem hard and cruel when living from crisis to crisis and when going back to easier times is preferred. Nonetheless, I could not go back at Kakum since the door was closed. I had to realize that the only thing from my past that I could carry ahead on the canopy was the memory of having been at the door of entrance and the wisdom I brought there with me. In fact, the door of entry itself is a divider from and a gateway to. It is factual: There is a canopy in the most beautiful of places on earth, and yet that very place is hell on earth. There is good and bad in Africa.

The second lesson of my Kakum experience is that Africa must deal with the hand life has dealt it, whether it assisted in its creation or someone else created it. As to the first it was I who decided that I wanted to go into the forest. It was I who decided where I wanted to live. It was I who decided which school I would attend and the career I would follow. And it is I who determined that this or that could and could not be done. I am the decision-maker in most of what does or does not happen in my life.

At the entrance of the forest I was asked if I wanted to go into the forest or remain behind. I decided to enter. In so doing I had moved from spectator to participant, from receiver to giver, from made to maker. In fact, Kakum will never be the same because I was there. It has been forever altered because I took that walk myself. In reporting on it, I have impacted constitutions for better or for worse. Kakum is partly my production. Its future is in our hands. Continental Ghanaians who had never been to Kakum were moved to go because of what I told them about the place. Kakum is my testimony.

Kakum's future has changed forever. I played my part in its future, it is hoped for good. However there is another fact of that forest. I neither created Kakum nor the canopy it contained. It was the work of the Great Other and others before me. Indeed others were there before me, and with my naked eyes I saw some of those others moving ahead of me on the very day I found the canopy to be so difficult and unfriendly. The point here is that some of what the trekkers created before me is horrifying. There is corruption and crime, misunderstanding and war, abject poverty and inordinate wealth, and fumbled freedom and mismanagement. I found it all in African worlds when I came to the forest. I wish things were not that way, and such was my wish vis-à-vis the canopy at Kakum.

When I came to terms with that factuality of Kakum I realized that no amount of wishing away would ever improve on what I thought should not be. I had to come face to face with my darkest hour – the fact that I could not just get off the canopy. It was then that I decided that the best thing to do was to move forward. Hope was ahead, not behind.

Kakum showed me that the trap of its canopy was both

my darkest and my finest hour. Darkest because I was now between a rock and a hard place; finest because my dawn began to rise in my darkest moments. Darkest because I was trapped; finest because I knew there was a way out, and that the ancestors had already traveled the road I was trying to take. Darkest because I stood there helpless, conceding the worst; finest because I remembered that Africans always said that God (Nyame, Ngai, Olorun, Mawu, etc.) helps those who help themselves. Thus Kakum's canopy was the finest hour because I began to deal with the hand life dealt me and found that life's problems could be solved.

In that spirit I went on ahead as directed by the wisdom of the gate and was lucky to come to one final point. In going ahead against great odds I learned that when communities work on life's problems within the boundaries of reasonableness, something can be accomplished. What I mean by "the boundaries of reasonableness" is "possibilities within bounds," i.e., within the limits of what is humanly possible for human beings to do in life. I mean what is natural or what can reasonably be expected of human beings.

Let me illustrate. Human beings cannot be expected to sprout wings and take to the sky like birds. A person may pray that such would happen, but it won't. To be sure, it's a waste of prayer and time to think that nature or God would accede to such desires or requests. This is what I mean by "the boundaries of reasonableness." In the case of Kakum it meant that I had some distance to go before the ordeal of the canopy would end. At the point of my extreme crisis I had six stations to go. It would not only have been unreasonable but quite stupid for me to think or psyche myself into believing that those stations did not exist, or that I could pray my way out of them. Literally, I had to pass through each station – one by one and step by step – if I ever expected to get beyond the trap in which I found myself. No fancy fix-its would work; and not even a miracle. I literally had to walk the distance myself. So, realizing what was before and what was true, I decided the best thing for me was to face the facts and start walking. I literally had to work my way through every obstacle. I had to confront and deal with every issue on my way to liberation, but each step towards liberation gave me more confidence to take the next one. By the time I got to the fourth juncture I could see the end. In fact, the end came early, perhaps halfway, and I coasted the rest of the distance.

Kakum showed me that there is enough in Africa's database and memory to push Africa forward in the most difficult of times. Its memory of life before the fall into disgrace, corruption, and carnage should take Africa beyond paralysis to action. Such memory allows for a sense of the best in the worst of times. It proclaims that justice is not only a subject of deep concern for African people but for others as well. Certainly it points to reservoirs of ancestral approaches and traditions in the search for life in seasons of death. In the push to move, reality is to be met and dealt with for what it really is in the struggle for freedom and a more just order. In the end ruptured conditions give way to a new order.

This vision of things will give impetus to matters discussed in Chapter Seven.

Notes

1. Henri Frankfort, *Ancient Egyptian Religion* (New York: Columbia University Press, 1948).
2. John S. Mbiti, *African Religions and Philosophy* (New York: Doubleday, 1969).
3. Basil Davidson, *The Black Man's Burden – Africa and the Curse of the Nation-State* (New York: Random House, Inc., 1992), p. 50.
4. Ibid., pp. 21-51.
5. Carter G. Woodson, *The History of the Negro Church* (3rd ed., Washington, D.C.: The Associated Publishers, 1972 [1921]), p. 23.
6. See George N. Ayittey, *Africa in Chaos* (New York: St. Martin's Press, 1998). I shall deal with the African-American side of this issue in Chapter Six.
7. Ibid., p. 50.
8. Ibid., p. 74.
9. Ibid., pp. 263-267.
10. Keith B. Richburg, *Out of America: A Black Man Confronts Africa* (New York: Harcourt Brace & Company, 1998).
11. Ibid., p. xv.
12. Ibid., p. 227.

CHAPTER SIX

The Nature of African Freedom in America

A year before his assassination, Martin Luther King, Jr. in his work *Where Do We Go From Here: Chaos or Community?*, wrote prophetically and programmatically about the need to adequately address the race problem.[1] For King segregation was problematic. It had effectively barred Africans in America from freely moving about in society and from social and economic opportunities accorded to whites as U.S. citizens. To reverse the situation King urged the government to install measures to ensure equality of opportunity for citizens of African descent. Equality of opportunity for African citizens in America would move America towards proper community, i.e., a color-blind society honoring the rights of all citizens regardless of skin tone.

In King's view such a society was a beloved community, but that community had been prevented from coming to full-bloom because of an entrenched segregationist code (segregation by race). The code mandated two Americas – one black and one white – and declared that they were equal. For King this was a fallacy in existence too long. To call attention to it King and his followers launched the Civil Rights Movement in the 1950s. Through sit-ins, marches, and legal challenges to segregation's ways, the movement exposed the pitfalls of the separate-but-equal dogma and challenged America to remove all impediments to the advancement of rights for African citizens.

However, the full import of the movement's challenge would be realized in the demands for human rights. Instead of focusing on rights of citizens as the Civil Rights Movement had in the 1950s and early 60s, the human rights drive of the mid-60s (and thereafter) focused on "rights to equality." King described the difference:

> 'For the vast majority of white Americans, the past decade – the first phase – had been a struggle to treat the Negro with a degree of decency, not of equality. White America was ready to demand that the Negro should be spared the lash of brutality and coarse degradation, but it had never been truly committed to helping him out of poverty, exploitation or all forms of discrimination. The outraged white citizen had been sincere when he snatched the whips from the Southern sheriffs and forbade them more cruelties. But when this was to a degree accomplished, the emotions that had momentarily inflamed him melted away. White Americans left the Negroes on the ground and in devastating numbers walked off with the aggressor.[2]

For King this behavior required human rights initiatives, to amend a long history of discrimination against America's African population. He alluded to their cost and focus:

> The real cost is ahead.... Jobs are harder and costlier to create than voting rolls. The eradication of slums housing millions is complex far beyond integrating buses and lunch counters.[3]

So, in prophetic style, King indicted white America for its shabby treatment of its African population. As prophet to a nation steep in misdeeds against Africans, King offered a plan of repentance. Failure to execute meant the nation's doom.

As to the first – white America's shabby treatment of its citizens of African descent – King urged whites to face up to past and current sins against African citizens in America. He stated:

> Let us take a look at the size of the problem through the lens of the Negro's status in 1967. When the Constitution was written, a strange formula to determine taxes and representation declared that the Negro was 60 percent of a person. Today another curious formula seems to declare he is 50 percent of a person. Of the good things in life he is approximately one-half those of whites; of the bad he has twice those of whites. Thus, half of all Negroes live in substandard housing, and Negroes have half the income of whites. When we turn to the negative experiences of life, the Negro has a double share. There are twice as many unemployed. The rate of infant mortality (widely accepted as an accurate index of general health) among Negroes is double that of whites. The equation pursues Negroes even into war. There are twice as many Negroes as whites in combat in Vietnam at the beginning of 1967, and twice as many Negro soldiers died in action (206 percent) in proportion to their numbers in the population.[4]

As to the second – a plan of correctives to compensate Africans citizens for deeds against them – King called for a mammoth national effort to wipe out inequality. He urged a federal program of jobs, housing, and education. In his view an undertaking of this type would demonstrate white America's penitence for centuries-old sins against citizens of African descent. It would serve as compensation for white sins against African citizens.

The federal government, in time, responded to King's challenge. It responded in the form of a head start program, a better chance, upward bound, fair and open housing, job training, equal employment opportunities, integrated schools, and affirmative action. These were measures the government used to atone for racial discrimination. They made possible an age of economic improvement for African citizens. Indeed Africans in America in greater numbers moved from economic despair to economic abundance, and from nothing to spare to superabundance in opportunities and resources. Africans in America became a part of great society hopes. Socially and economically Africans in America played their part in ensuring that America would be an indivisible, multicultural society. This was viewed as progress under the terms of integration. However, King warned about economic progress without social and moral duty:

> The stability of the large world house which is ours will involve a revolution of values to accompany the scientific and freedom revolutions engulfing the world. We must rapidly begin the shift from a "thing"-oriented society to a "person"-oriented society. When machines and computers, profit motives and property rights are considered more important than people, the giant triplets of racism, materialism and militarism are incapable of being conquered. A civilization can flounder as readily in the face of moral and spiritual bankruptcy as it can through financial bankruptcy.[5]

King was not speaking to the wind in this warning. Rather he spoke to Africans in America, to would-be beneficiaries of human rights opportunities. In a prophetic tone he warned them of the danger of Black Power (economic ability and clout) when such power is not tempered by a sense of moral duty. King said:

> Some Black Power advocates consider an appeal to

conscience irrelevant. A Black Power exponent said to me not long ago: "To hell with conscience and morality. We want power." But power and morality must go together, implementing, fulfilling and ennobling each other. In the quest for power I cannot by-pass the concern for morality. I refuse to be driven to a Machiavellian cynicism with respect to power. Power at its best is the right use of strength. The words of Alfred the Great are still true: "Power is never good unless he who has it is good."[6]

Hence, with this perspective on power serving as a philosophical gauge for future black-white relations and for decision-making in the human rights struggle, King directed Africans in America to choose moral values over skin color. He called for a coalition of blacks and whites of good will to work on civil and human rights issues. He thought that Black Power was an impediment to a beloved community of citizens of good will working together across racial lines. King asserted:

> Black Power alone is no more insurance against social injustice than white power. Negro politicians can be as opportunistic as their white counterparts if there is not an informed and determined constituency demanding social reform. What is most needed is a coalition of Negroes and liberal whites that will work to make both major parties truly responsive to the needs of the poor. Black Power does not envision or desire such a program.[7]

As if to telecast the inevitable when power is not anchored in spiritual values King added:

> But many middle-class Negroes have forgotten their roots and are more interested in "conspicuous consumption" than about the cause of justice. Instead, they seek to sit in some serene and passionless realm of isolation, untouched and unmoved by the ago-

nies and struggles of their underprivileged brothers.
This kind of selfish detachment has caused the
masses of Negroes to feel alienated not only from
white society but also from the Negro middle class.
They feel that the average middle-class Negro has
no concern for their plight.[8]

Some twenty-six years later Cornel West would recast
King's warning as prophetic and moral reasoning.[9] However,
between King's time (1967) and the beginning of this new
century (the twenty-first century) would develop an over-
flowing tide of what Black Power (economic ability) became
under integration in the African world. The remainder of this
chapter will delineate that saga – especially what freedom
becomes when it is fueled by a "let us catch up" philosophy
rather than by ethnic duty in oppressive circumstances. It
relates what freedom's results have been for African America
since the 1960s. In a word, it will show that freedom (under
the civil and human rights banner) became a co-opting project. Indeed, freedom in integration stripped Africans in
America of their moral sense and their spirit of otherness in
America and the world. Its route led Africans from segregation to desegregation to disintegration and finally to incorporation in the white world to benefit that world. The final
chapter will call for the rectification of this problem and for
a redefinition and redirection for African freedom in America
and in the world.

Defining African Freedom in America

A. THE LOSERS' PERSPECTIVE

In debating with Black Power advocates in 1967, Martin
Luther King Jr. waxed eloquently about the unfortunate use
of the Black Power slogan. Yet King recognized that Black
Power advocates had been prophetic, for they had the courage
to speak to deep longings of the masses for meaningful power.
Recognizing their pain, King posited:

For people who had been crushed so long by white

power and who had been taught that black was degrading, it had a ready appeal.[10]

Nonetheless, King, for the sake of his *coalition building goal,* went on to underscore his reservation about the language. He told its advocates that the concept had denotative as well as connotative meanings in cultural usage:

> While the concept of legitimate Black Power might be denotatively sound, the slogan "Black Power" carried the wrong connotations. I mentioned the implications of violence that the press had already attached to the phrase. And I went on to say that some of the rash statements on the part of a few marchers only reinforced this impression.[11]

Hence, Black Power for King and Black Power advocates meant one thing and for white America quite another. For Black Power advocates it meant the power of black people to work on and take care of black issues without white interference and with little or no white assistance. It meant black people controlling their labor and resources and mining their independence. For whites (in King's view) it suggested a reduction of their power. It was sharing their power with black people.

Whites in America would say no to Black Power as defined by Black Power advocates and African masses. While civil rights was not a big problem for whites (indeed it increased their economic holdings), Black Power – it seemed to most whites – was. Its advocates did call for an increase in economic holdings for black benefits. For excluded and oppressed African masses economic power was salvation. It meant a chance to live in a world owned and operated by African people for the benefit of African people. It signaled the end of seducers and the rebirth of collective identity. It meant freedom from white control.

Freedom, for Black Power advocates, was black parity in the world of economic exchange. It meant black cultural nationalism without the restraints of segregation. It meant African schools owned and operated by African people with African administrators and teachers in charge. It meant African people working on African issues. In radical nationalist circles it meant separatism, i.e., freedom *to be* without white interference.

This kind of freedom was not the kind that Africans integrationists wanted. This type reminded them of segregation. It was the freedom of losers.

B) THE WINNERS' PERSPECTIVE

Chiseled as it was out of segregation and responses to racial restrictions, freedom looked different for the non-nationalist Africans, who were guided by integrationist objectives. For this group, freedom more often meant turning to the white world for what the black world needed. It meant leaving black projects to work on white projects.

A peculiar psychology fueled this view of freedom. Banned by rules of slavery and segregation from access to and free movement in white worlds for centuries, freedom offered integrationist Africans a pass to forbidden spaces. Freedom meant the opportunity of going where one always wanted to go in the white world, of doing what one always wanted to do.... It meant unhindered movement, and here unhindered movement was the freedom to circulate, participate, and make a living in worlds created and controlled by white America.

An African staff-colleague of mine, for instance, confirmed this point in stating that freedom for her meant "an uncluttered existence." A colleague professor asserted that freedom was "exercising options without undue restraints." For another colleague it meant "the ability to determine for one's self the lifestyle one would pursue." For several continental and diaspora African students it meant, among others, "unrestrained being," "one's natural state." Thus, freedom is the unhindered state. For integrationist-minded Africans that state is the chance to do what one has been forbidden to do – full membership and full participation in white worlds.

Orlando Patterson helps us to see how such perspectives

on freedom fit under the Western gaze. Of the three types of freedom he mentions – personal, sovereignal, and civic – the statements by my colleagues and students seem to fall within the range of the first two.[12] Patterson's first category (personal freedom) is likely to be exhibited in my colleague's "uncluttered existence" thinking, that is, "not being coerced or restrained by anyone in doing something desired, and, on the other hand the conviction that one can do as one pleases within the limits of the other person's desire to do the same." Patterson's sovereignal freedom is "the power to act as one pleases, regardless of the wishes of others...." My colleague's view that 'freedom is one's ability to determine what one's style should be and pursue that style' is perhaps nearest to Patterson's sovereignal freedom. Patterson's third type of freedom (civic freedom) is "the capacity of adult members of a community to participate in its life and governance," which in some communities, as suggested by Patterson, may mean adult (and in some cases elite) males only.

However, most insightful for my thesis is Patterson's view of how the idea of freedom and being free became an obsession of Western culture. He posits that the meaning of freedom, in Western tradition, was largely determined by slavery:

> Slavery is the permanent, violent and personal domination of natally alienated and generally dishonored persons. It is, first, a form of personal domination. One individual is under the direct power of another or his agent. In practice, this usually entails the power of life and death over the slave. Second, the slave is always an excommunicated person. He, more often she, does not belong to the legitimate social or moral community; he has no independent social existence; he exists only through, and for, the master; he is, in other words, natally alienated.[13]

By analogy, then, one might say that the long years of African excommunicated existence in America not only forged a definition of freedom for America; it gave most Africans, (the African majority), their vision of freedom as well. In other words freedom for the non-nationalist African majority in America is unhindered *access to and opportunities in the white world.*

African Freedom in Context

The standard view of most writers on African history is that the first persons of African descent in America came to Jamestown, Virginia, in 1619. Of importance for some writers also is the fact that the Jamestown group did not voluntarily come to America, as did Europeans, nor did their African relatives who followed them for centuries thereafter. Instead, Africans were brought to North America against their will from 1619 until the end of the African Slave Trade in 1807. Thereafter, the domestic slave trade was legally practiced in North America until the end of the Civil War (1865). Legal segregation, another form of enslavement, followed in the 1890s and endured in the American south until 1971.

Enslavement conflicted with the African way of life. Consequently, Africans in America could not and did not make peace with an enslaved status. Evidence for their nonacceptance of enslavement is found in the constant need of European settlers to develop rules and regulations for "the better ordering of slaves" as early as the 1660s. The aim of such rules (slave codes) was to regulate enslaved Africans in religious and secular affairs and to make sure that the enslaved African would be at the mercy of their slaveholders in every possible way. For example, there was the rule regarding legal status. If an enslaved mother gave birth to a child, the child – like the mother – was an enslaved person for life. A master from a slave state in the United States could recover a runaway slave from any state, by custom and practice. Other regulations forbade African cultural traditions and practices on plantations and in other settings, e.g., there were rules against African drumming, ritual observances, and African religious practices. Then there were customary regulations, for example: An African enslaved person had no right that a white person had to respect. In time, with a fading memory and connection with Africa and an African past, these regulations not only made the enslaved more dependent on whites for life and limb; African hopes and aspirations shifted from Afrocentric to Eurocentric ones.

Africans in these circumstances recognized that their futures were in the hands of their more powerful and impressive slavelords. To that end slaveholders added to slave codes a system of remuneration that was based on whether an African had or had not adjusted to Eurocentric expectations. Enslaved persons demonstrating that they had adjusted and reported or kept in check those who had not were rewarded with promotions and perks. For example, a cooperative enslaved person could move up to slave driver, or to a position in the big house, or to other privileges. Those who showed little or no progress or resisted the culture of the slaveholding system were demoted to ever worsening conditions. To the latter belonged floggings, threats to be sold, transfers to far worse circumstances, dismemberment, and even death.

In time Christianity – *properly taught* – took up this trajectory and became a most potent weapon for "the better ordering of slaves," offering rewards to those who towed its expectations and punishments to those who did not. As such many Africans in America opting for sanctuary from the tyranny of the slaveholding system and hell in the afterlife became Methodists, Baptists, Presbyterians, Catholics, and Episcopalians. In so doing, they unwittingly chose to be measured by religious traditions and customs of the slaveholding white world, made all the more attractive by the institutionalizing of white supremacy in human chain theories and the thinking of Charles Darwin on the origin of species. In that thinking African people were viewed as savages on the first ledge of the ladder of civilization. Resultantly, such conditions imbued most with the idea that the white world at the top was far more attractive and profitable than the black world at the bottom. Thus freedom came to mean privileges within the white world.

The above factors and descriptions underscore why Africans in America have constructed their images of freedom in the way they have today. Freedom's desires and aspirations grew out of an African desire to be accepted by whites in America. As people without freedom and power, freedom meant the power to be like and do what white folks did. By the turn of the twentieth century, the African scholar W.E.B. Dubois describes the outcome of the process as follows:

> After the Egyptian and Indian, the Greek and Roman, the Teuton and the Mongolian, the Negro is a sort of seventh son, born with a veil, and gifted with second-sight in this American world, - a world which yields him no true self-consciousness, but only lets him see himself through the revelation of the other world. It is a peculiar sensation, this double-consciousness, this sense of always looking at one's self through the eyes of others, of measuring one's soul by the tape of a world that looks on in amused contempt and pity. One ever feels his twoness, - an American, a Negro; two souls, two thoughts, two unreconciled strivings; two warring ideals in one dark body, whose dogged strength alone keeps it from being torn asunder.[14]

Psychologically then, the scene is not a laudable one. In the post-civil rights period (1970s and thereafter) Dubois' two souls issued into a single one – an *American African* who is part and parcel of the white world. Here freedom means a life that is not under the guardianship of African community regulations and expectations. Indeed, it is an exodus from black to white worlds. It is the habits and peculiarities of mainstream white America. It is the African in America cut off from history and an African-centered focus. It is the life of a future that is not determined by the lessons of the past. It is living under the regulations of a world created by white America and for white America. It is antiancestral.

Free at Last

The freedom campaigns of the 1960s and 70s encouraged a large number of Africans in America to leave traditional African communities and seek their fortune in the white world. It generated an exodus initiated by the African middle class. That class not only invaded the white world in search for opportunities; it became primary beneficiaries of the sweat and blood of human rights results – thanks to the Civil Rights Acts of 1964, the Voters Rights Act of 1965, and the Housing Act of 1968. It benefited because the rewards of civil and human rights depended on the password *money,* which the poor did not have. The poor African masses remained, in the words of Derrick Bell, "faces at the bottom of the well."

Entering doors the masses pried open the middle class became large buffer zones separating white society from the masses. In fact, middle-class Africans often became go-between experts on the masses to the larger world. Some would declare war against the masses and make careers out of the bell curve views. Others became baptized believers in the religion of integration and chief spokespersons for its doctrines and principles. Sitting among those who preached and reveled in the gospel of greed, they viewed the enormity of their acquisition as heavenly signs of divine favor. Their moral breath was shortened by the asthma of portfolios. Money and more money, things and more things became their God. The masses, however, would languish in poverty and rot before their eyes.

Listening to William Julius Wilson

Middle-class Africans in America, spurred on by benefits of civil and human rights, unwittingly became contributors to problems the masses faced in inner-city neighborhoods and in other contexts in the 1970s and 80s. The possibility of this assessment first simmered in the attack sociologist Julius Wilson launched in 1987 against conservative social scientists who argued that the problems of African masses in America's urban areas were generated by African ghetto dwellers them-

selves.[15] Wilson showed that inner city African ghetto problems began in the mid-60s with the sudden increase in crime
rate (violent and property crimes), teenage pregnancy, female-
headed families, drug addition, and welfare dependency... in
that sector. Wilson stated:

> ...one quarter of all black births occurred outside
> of marriage in 1965... and by 1980 57 percent
> were; in 1965 nearly 25 percent of all black fami-
> lies were headed by women, and by 1980 43 per-
> cent were, partly as a result welfare dependency
> among the poor blacks has mushroomed. And per-
> haps the most dramatic indicator of the extent to
> which social dislocations have afflicted urban blacks
> is crime, especially violent crime, which has
> increased sharply in recent years. Finally, these
> growing social problems have accompanied increas-
> ing black rates of joblessness.[16]

As a means of explaining these dire statistics Wilson went
on to show that the appearance of these debilitating conditions related to the fact that the urban African masses (the
underclass) in America had not been gainfully employed since
the 1960s. According to Wilson, when America (and the
world) shifted from a production economy to a high-tech
service one in the 1960s, poor Africans with no skills (and
without money and talent) became defenseless. Wilson theo-
rized that when there is no work and income, or legitimate
ways of obtaining work and income, socially unacceptable
behavior develops and feeds upon itself. Thus genetic inferiority as the cause for dysfunctional behavior among blacks of
the inner cities, as conservative social scientists had argued, is
baseless for Wilson. Rather the real cause behind ghetto dysfunctional behaviors is a lack of employment opportunities
and productive engagements among inner-city urban dwellers.

Wilson augmented his thesis by showing that the mid-60s
behavior of inner-city ghetto dwellers began at the time when
middle-class Africans in America exited inner-city neighbor-

hoods for the suburbs. Prior to the time the presence and style of this class in inner-city neighborhoods, according to Wilson, reminded poor residents what the larger society expected of citizens. However, the middle-class exodus left ghetto neighborhoods without such models. Later Wilson illustrated:

> Indeed, in the 1940s and 1950s, and as late as the 1960s such communities featured a vertical integration of different segments of the urban black population. Lower-class, working-class, and middle-class black families all lived more or less in the same communities (albeit in different neighborhoods), sent their children to the same schools, availed themselves of the same recreational facilities, and shopped at the same stories. Whereas today's black middle-class professionals no longer tend to live in ghetto neighborhoods and have moved increasingly into mainstream occupations outside the black community, the black middle-class professionals of the 1940s and 1950s (doctors, teachers, lawyers, social workers, ministers) lived in higher-income neighborhoods of the ghetto and serviced the black community. Accompanying the black middle-class exodus has been a growing movement of stable working-class blacks from the ghetto neighborhoods to the higher-income neighborhoods in other parts of the city and to the suburbs... their very presence provided stability to inner-city neighborhoods and reinforced and perpetuated mainstream patterns of norms and behavior.[17]

Later Wilson illustrated his thesis by putting the urban African ghetto situation on stage, telling the world its story in its own words.[18] In so doing, Wilson was able to show that African urban dwellers of the ghetto had the same aspirations as their civil-righting ancestors – gainful employment to avoid becoming social statistics and parasites on the system. To that end Wilson called for a unified force to address the needs of the African poor:

> Because the problems of the ghetto joblessness are so severe and because they are associated with social problems that make many of our central cities increasingly unattractive places in which to reside and work, a vision of interracial unity that acknowledges distinctively racial problems but nonetheless emphasizes common solutions to common problems is more important now than ever. Such a vision should be developed, shared, and promoted by leaders in this country, but especially by political leaders.[19]

However, Wilson's analysis and critique were designed to help public policy decision-makers to focus on real issues, not contrived ones for political advantage as conservative social scientists did in assessing the case of the African poor. To that end Wilson is to be commended for rescuing the predicament of real people from the politics of the bell curve. In the key of social scientists Wilson's task was one of posting facts and offering theses in light of facts. He made no interethnic evaluation of the forays of the exiting African middle class into white worlds for opportunities. He made no judgement about whether it was good or bad to give up self-reliance in the black world for dependency in the white world. He gave no warning of what wealth without morals could become as King had in 1967. As such, Wilson speaks for bourgeois interests and integrationist habits.

Freedom Among the Freed

Because social scientists like Wilson have focused so much on the problems of the African poor in America – their abnormal state of life as compared to the middle class – and what is required to fix their situation, the habits of upwardly mobile Africans have hardly been critiqued. Perhaps this is because it is typical to think that white racist ways made the black world what it is today. Nevertheless, this is a non-African perspective as I have shown in Chapter Two. For that reason I believe that African history-making is now up for review. The rest of this chapter focuses on such a review.

My review is guided by the following premise: *Africans in America created the predicament they are in and must accept blame for it.* I say this not only because traditionally the African view comes to terms with personal and communal ailments. I say this because Africans in America have essentially been in charge of their destiny since Rosa Parks provided the spark that ignited the modern freedom movement in the white-only section of a Montgomery, Alabama, bus in 1954. Since that time, more than forty years ago, Africans in America have become privileged citizens with degrees from Stanford, Penn, Columbia, Yale, Duke, Harvard, Boston University, University of Chicago, University of Alabama, University of Mississippi, etc. Indeed, much time has passed since Africans had technical and vocational training opportunities and benefited from good jobs and good salaries. In fact, great numbers changed addresses since the 1950s; and great numbers have become persons of means. Statistics show that Africans in America have not only survived, but that a sizeable number are economically well-off.[20] But to what end are these benefits?

This query goes to the heart of the freedom question and how Africans in America of means view freedom today. For me the freedom script of Africans in America does not read well. In general freedom has meant the chance to move up and away from African concepts, African issues, African values, African survival strategies, and African communities, socially and emotionally. It has meant a chance to trade in modest means for plutocratic splurging and to move away from a common life of sharing to ostentatious individualism. It has meant an opportunity to measure self-worth by the depth of one's pockets. It has meant things and more things. It has meant pain and failure to which few would dare admit.

Freedom results accrue when freedom means individuated

existence. It often means live wherever one wants to live, work wherever one wants to work, spend money wherever one wishes, be with whomever one wants to be with, and ask few if any moral questions. Here freedom is both color-blind and issue-blind. It means getting rich by any means necessary, saying nothing controversial, being politically correct, and doing what "successful" citizens do. It means acting without thinking and benefiting without doing. Freedom means to be preoccupied with personal pleasure.

Major black magazines in America never cease to remind us of this kind of freedom. Their function, as is true of all magazines, is to offer subscribers and readers what matters most to them. If my premise is correct, then black magazines print what African readers in America (their main subscription holders) are really interested in – money and more money and what money can do for black folk. While one can find subjects other than money-related ones in black magazines, their objective is to satisfy the monetary concerns of their clientele. Accordingly, some preach the gospel of Africans who have homes too large to live in, who own cars too fancy and luxurious to ever drive on public highways, who go to the most exquisite places on earth to visit, who purchase clothes too costly to wear. For instance, the November 2000 issue of *Ebony* devoted twenty pages in sequence to "New Cars for 2001." And the others follow *Ebony* in one way or another.

It is difficult to blame *Ebony* and other black magazines for these ostentatious displays. As business ventures they offer what interests their clientele. If this is true, then Africans in America of means are interested in living the high life. In fact, a life of luxury is touted by some as "delay of gratification awards," which their ancestors never got because of racial discrimination. These awards are often viewed as *good salaries and buying power*. However, good salaries are not used wisely in most cases. For example, an African annual income of $40 billion at the time of Dr. King's death in 1968 rose to "$324 billion in 1995 from $304.5 billion in 1994."[21] But what kind of fruit did the increase bear? Statistics tell us that

...Black households spent $10.8 billion in 1995 on new cars and trucks, which is a 156 percent increase from the year before. The average Black household spends $1,592 a year on clothing compared to $1,650 a year for Whites. Blacks outspent Whites by nearly 10 percent when it came to clothing for children under 15. Blacks spend 48 percent more than whites on food prepared at home.[22]

Here one wonders if Africans in America will follow the same path with a $500 billion plus income at the beginning of this century?

The tendency to engage in ostentatious consumerism and self-promotion seems pandemic since the 1960s. In this behavior black athletes lead the way. While it is common knowledge, for instance, that Africans in America are 13 percent of the population, they held 80 percent of the playing slots in the National Basketball Association in the late 1990s. In the period research also showed that NBA salaries ranged from a low of $247,000 to double-digit millions. Similar high salaries were also being paid to black baseball and football players. Furthermore, some received supplemental salaries - megabucks endorsement contracts. For example, Nike was known to have paid Michael Jordan in the period more than $40 million to advertise its product. And currently big business has the earning power of Jordan for the 2001–2002 NBA season.

What is the public persona of these well-off athletes? Simply put, ostentatious splurging and scheming. For example, a $40 million contract with Nike wooed millions of financially-strapped blacks into Nike's camp – I mean poor blacks from inner-city neighbors – to fly high like Mike for shoe prices far beyond their means.[23] As a result, many young black males dream of becoming star athletes with the wealth and flare of their athletic heroes. Yet all they will ever do in that regard is overload the coffers of sneaker empires like Nike by purchasing their products. This is a case of African superstars misusing their influence, robbing the poor to benefit the rich;

sadder still is the fact that they do not own the empires they make and promote.

This spirit in African communities goes beyond sports. The same population of 13 percent of America's total is said to buy 26 percent of the Cadillac cars sold each year. Furthermore, Africans in America of means often convene "feast of fools" summer conventions without rhyme or reason, except perhaps for lavish enjoyment. Millions of dollars are spent on goods and services at hotels and getaways, with few benefits reaching African nonconventioneers back home. If these middle-class conventioneers (the main staple of these conventions) and their organizers do benefit from their ostentatious escapades, they pass the proceeds on to patrons (usually whites proprietors) who provided them space and board to revel in undisciplined conduct. Seldom do these conventioneers return to their constituencies with more than empty pockets and brain-dead heads. This is because freedom for too many means splurging. It means money and the right to enjoy.

Judging Freedom Results

The preceding habits and practices show the unfortunate direction freedom takes when people bereft of freedom view its acquisition as permission to do uncritically what they could not do before. It not only shows a predilection for reveling in personal pleasure and ostentatious living without regard for poorer individuals of the community. It negatively affects the poor. What I mean is that poor Africans in America tend to view the upwardly mobile among them as examples to imitate. More often this means following their footsteps with expensive automobiles, expensive clothing, and nonessential luxury items. However, without money to support the habits they see in their more able sisters and brothers, they are sometimes drawn into a life of crime to realize them.

What then is my judgement? It is simply this: When freedom's goals in African worlds are colored by a philosophy of individual accomplishment rather than by the measure of collective progress, freedom can create unnecessary suffering for the community as a whole. In traditional thinking the sufferings that Africans experience today throughout the world are African created – signs of ancestral displeasure with African worlds – and can only be remedied when infractions cease. The great infraction that stands in need of removal in African worlds today is the freedom that rings without a collective sound, i.e., individuated freedom. That is the freedom of suffering and tragedy since moral duty is missing. The point is that under this kind of freedom, i.e., freedom forged by jail-break preconditioning, excluded people (once freed) can conduct themselves in ways that do not honor ancestral intention. They can destroy what marks them as a people and so destroy themselves. For this reason freedom for Africans often seems like the caged let loose on a smorgasbord of opportunity without definition and restraint. Barred from eating so long, eating too often becomes an obsession. The quality of the food becomes a nonissue.

A story exhibiting this critique appeared in a major American magazine regarding some African women who made it their business to frequent Asians fingernail shops despite deepening social problems between Asians and Africans in America. Of that relation it was stated:

> The Vietnamese employees assiduously pamper blacks, who don't often feel that society is rushing to lay soft hands upon them. How bad could relations be in a place where someone holds your hands for an hour, then gives you a mini-massage before you go, all without breaking a $20 bill?[24]

The point is this: When a group has been denied privileges for a long time an undue focus on what is denied can override sensitivity to issues that require a more critical or prophetic response. Here a prophetic response is an ancestral one. It is that which the community calls upon for direction when pressing needs would cause it to veer off course for quick fixes or temporary advantages. In this case the fingernail pleasure seekers sacrificed ancestral principles because personal enjoyment – the need to have their nails done by some one other than themselves – upstaged their duty to stay away from Asian fingernail shops until conflict between the Asian and African communities had been adequately addressed and resolved. Freedom, in this case, became the fulfillment of individual desire; the choice to buy what money could buy without moral scruples or community directions. Freedom meant the right to engage indiscriminately.

When any group travels the freedom road in this way it leaves nonexemplary portraits for its progeny once it is gone. For Africans in America what is lost is resiliency in the storm through acceptance and promotion of a culture of communalism. That culture helped Africans survive the hard life of slavery and segregation. Today not only is that culture lost, but the sense of what is right and wrong is lost too. If a culture is lost, a people is lost.

A lot more is lost however. As a people preoccupied with personal success at any cost Africans lost their innocence. Like white America's hands African hands today are stained with the blood of the innocent near and far over the last forty years. Simon of Cyrene, Jesus' helper in the cross scene, is no longer an African in America as he was for James Weldon Johnson in 1927. Then (1927) Africans in America stood apart from those who slaughtered the innocent. Integrationist habits made Africans in America co-conspirators in the slaughter. Greed and empire seeking became preoccupations. How could it be otherwise? It is no fiction: Africans in America have fewer spaces to grow independence and promote their values and culture, diminished as they are from approximately 15 million acres of land in 1912 to less than 6 million at the beginning of the third millennium. So no longer custodians of African destiny – with hospitals, restaurants, hotels, shops, farms, schools, religion, memories, ancestral values – Africans in America are vulnerable to and trapped in a system of their own making.

Thus freedom means debt (enslavement) to Euro-American systems and values. The ancestral freedom as freedom from debt to the system in slavery and segregation is now freedom to make payments for TVs stationed in each room of the mansion, for BMWs and Mercedes Benz that line driveways, and for $400 thousand mortgages to banks stretching over thirty years on average. I hold that debt is a disease that strangles the moral voice. It strangles the call to duty. It clips the wings of mercy and justice.

Under the conditions of debt college and university professors of African descent who teach in integrated systems cannot teach what they know and can teach. Rather they become bards of state and private interests. Some under these conditions portend radicalism, but their radicalism is basically conversations of the mind designed for intellectual stimulation and amusement. They talk and theorize about justice but cannot do justice. In fact, if they were to teach and do justice the systemic trap in which they are held would quash the last bit of life out of them. For that reason these professors are more likely to make spin-off comments about what mainstream society defines as contemporary issues. They are paid to teach a certain kind of truth, not to make judgements. And so rather than run the risk of being current and truthful these professors either specialize in what has been or veer off into imagination.

Let me illustrate the point. The former (specializing in what has been) is what I call a scholarship of literary archeology, i.e., the knack for digging in old piles as a sure way of keeping one from making comments on current issues (for such would not be accepted in the academy as scholastic). In my own field (New Testament and Christian Origins) I would call this the scholarship of biblical archeology. That scholarship says much about back yonder but almost nothing about right now. It believes in digging up and reconfiguring centuries-old bones but never speaking about current ones. The latter (veering off into imagination) is the tendency of some to hide from reality and personal risk by entering into the safe haven of writing fiction. This becomes an interesting way of amusing the mind and the spirit without standing up and being counted for anything in the real world. Either way, little is said about pressing issues of the world today. No first aid or service is ever given to communities and peoples that are oppressed. Nothing is said about environmental issues. Scholarship becomes an exercise in irrelevancy – thanks to integration.

Far more disconcerting (and I would say dangerous because of the proclivity of African people for the spiritual) is the fascination that so many middle-class Africans have had for the trappings of integrationist religion in the last three decades. Throughout the civil and human rights campaigns (from the 1950s – 1980s) let-out-of-the-cage religionists within the African world led African communities on a guilt trip by use of the old Hellenistic religious adage "out of many the one." To ensure that Africans in America would become one with the white world these religionists anchored their objective on a one-blood thesis they believed was biblical, and therefore divine. Using the biblical text of Acts 17:26 (a New Testament text) they determined that it was divine duty to institutionalize the thesis through interracial committees, interracial communions, and so on. Integrationist priests and priestesses bellowed that Sunday morning was the most segregated hour in America. What they never realized is that the one God, one blood, one faith thesis was originally promoted in a social context where some individuals were seeking a decided advantage over their adversaries. Those seeking hegemony used the thesis to support their politics. They never admitted that in the Bible itself the thesis is no more or less than the word of a minority to a majority. It was really about how a minority sought to secure its position in the world by calling the majority to convert to a new way of thinking about life. The thesis was about conquest. It was the way Christians of the early church world positioned themselves to gather the spoils of the world's greatest missionary, Alexander the Great. It was he who first called for a one-world, one-blood, multicultural order as a way of positioning Europe to acquire wealth and power beyond its borders.

This Alexander was the progenitor of Western civilization. This civilization, rooted as it was in poverty, made a dash for the world's resources armed with global imagination and military might. It called for a one-world order guided by its language and condiments of culture. To that end it cemented its project by its bandages of philosophy and religion. It divided the world into the civilized and uncivilized, rewarding the converted from among the uncivilized with citizenship and privilege but with no real power. Those who refused incorporation into its plans, i.e., did not submit to its grandiose aims, were hung out to dry.

The duty of those who did submit was to campaign for the Hellenistic way and to ensure that all converts become promoters and ambassadors of its hegemonic goals. The conquered (like their Hellenistic masters) would not only think in conquistador terms; they became high priests and ministers of its systems. In time they would exhibit little compassion for the poor and would know nothing of prophecy. How could they when they measured their own progress as well as the progress of the people by Hellenistic norms such as their houses, positions, mainstream education, "first positions" in the society of their rulers, and so on?

Thus, in the same way African priests and priestesses in America became leaders in oppressive and indiscriminate conduct, not remembering that religion's primary concern is to make the crooked straight and to live outside the camp. Traditionally, they thought of themselves as living torches of divine responsibility calling for light in dark places and for justice among the unjust, but infected by the germ of integration and its benefits they drifted away from this mandate and failed miserably in their duties. The end result is that the oppressed became oppressors in continental and diaspora African worlds. The masses in both contexts began to live in poverty while the middle-class leadership feasted in the house of Belshazzar. In Africa debt and indebtedness to Europeans in the forms of loans from European and American companies and from the IMF and the World Bank became a divine way. Africa as a whole became a system of neocolonial nations. In the U.S. freedom gave way to bank mortgages, to long-term notes to finance companies for automobiles and other amenities, and to patronage systems for jobs. Added to this is the statistic showing that the high life that Africans in America live today would end within one month if their white-controlled jobs were eliminated.[25]

Hence African freedom on the continent and in the diaspora is tantamount to enslavement to the very world from which Africans sought liberation from in the 1950s and 60s. For that reason the African moral voice throughout the world has whittled to a whimper these days. Fewer claim to see or hear anything about abuse and injustice in the world – a common tactic used when people surrender their moral and cultural sense. Notwithstanding, brush fires stirred by oppression still burn. Could this be because systems of incorporation and integration controlled from afar virtually own African people everywhere – their lands, houses, cars, wives, husbands, children, schools, churches, lives, ministers, teachers? And even more disconcerting is that the nations of the world that formerly viewed Africans in America in particular as *the not guilty* may now have good reasons to second-guess their judgement. It may be that because of the increasing indebtedness of Africans to people of European descent in the last thirty-five to forty years, oppressed peoples now view Africans as servants and promoters of oppressive systems? Perhaps oppressed groups think that Africans work as spies and as assistants for the powers that press them down and threaten their future? Perhaps the bombings in East Africa were a cry from the oppressed to the oppressed to remember its heritage? If those bombings do speak of the expendability of a once-oppressed people who decided to take the side of oppressors, then they invite the previously oppressed-turn-oppressors to return to roots of responsible life – compassion for the disallowed and a liberation of nonruptured life.

Notes

1. Martin Luther King, Jr., *Where Do We Go From Here: Chaos or Community?* (Boston: Beacon Press, 1967).
2. Ibid., pp. 3-4.
3. Ibid., pp. 5-6.
4. Ibid., pp. 6-7.
5. Ibid., p. 186.
6. Ibid., p. 59.
7. Ibid., p. 49.
8. Ibid., pp. 131-132.
9. See Cornel West, *Race Matters* (Boston: Beacon Press, 1993), especially the chapters on "The Pitfalls of Racial Reasoning" and "The Crisis of Black Leadership," pp. 21-32 and 33-46, respectively.
10. King, *Where Do We Go From Here?*, p. 29.
11. Ibid., p. 30.
12. Orlando Patterson, *Freedom: Freedom in the Making of Western Culture* (San Francisco: HarperCollins Publishers, 1991), pp. 3-4.
13. Ibid., pp. 9-10.
14. W.E.B. DuBois, *The Souls of Black Folk* (1903. Reprint; New York: The Blue Heron Press, 1953), p. 3.
15. William Julius Wilson, *The Truly Disadvantaged: The Inner City, the Underclass and Public Policy* (Chicago and London: The University of Chicago Press, 1987).
16. Ibid., p. 20. These statistics do not signify that Africans of the underclass in America are a degenerate group as Herrnstein and Murray [See Richard J. Herrnstein and Charles Murray, *The Bell Curve: Intelligence and Class Structure in American Life* (New York: The Free Press, 1994)] would later claim. They argued that the social maladies of the ghetto demonstrate the genetic inferiority of Africans in America, and that government fix-it programs, such as those of the Great Society initiatives, were a waste of national resources. They also claim that the situation and condition of Africans of the ghetto is the clearest indication that the genetically inferior did not and would not benefit from government assistance. "Blacks on welfare" is pointed to as a public example of this thesis and therefore the new emphasis on welfare to work at the beginning of the new century.
17. Ibid., p. 7.
18. William Julius Wilson, *When Work Disappears: The World of the New Urban Poor* (New York: Vintage Books, 1996).
19. Ibid., p. xxi.
20. See Orlando Patterson, *The Ordeal of Integration: Progress and Resentment in America's "Racial" Crisis* (Washington, D.C.: Civitas/Counterpoint, 1997), pp. 17-27.
21. *Jet* (September 9, 1996): 90/17:40.

22. Ibid.
23. See *U.S. News and World Report* (March 24, 1997): 122/11:46-52.
24. See "Racial Fingernail Politics: Blacks and Asians Find a Strange Harmony at the Beauty Shop," by Debra Dickerson *News and World U.S Report* (April 14, 1997): 122/14:33-35).
25. See Melvin H. Oliver and Thomas M. Shapiro, *Black Wealth/White Wealth: A Perspective on Racial Inequality* (New York and London: Routledge, 1995), pp. 96-97.

CHAPTER SEVEN

African Freedom and Liberation in America

For Africans in America burdened by restrictions of enslavement for more than two centuries and legal segregation for almost another, freedom became associated with unhindered movement. It was a jailbreak from the confines of segregation and a grand entrance into worlds of centuries-old white privileges. The 60s marked my own jailbreak. I willfully decided to enter a white-only waiting room at a doctor's office in my hometown to ascertain whether segregation existed beyond the stipulation of law. It still did. Before I could seat myself comfortably in that waiting room, I was whisked away by the doctor's nurse without explanation. The only statement she made to me on the way out of that white-only waiting room was "the doctor will see you now." I got to see the doctor ahead of what seemed like twenty white patients and a host of black patients in the "colored" waiting room – yet I knew the score. I had violated the rules of "white-only" spaces. Thereafter, I made a career out of violating those spaces.

In the process of my frequent violations a shift of focus had begun to take place. I found myself more and more in spaces outside of all-African reserves, and the more I entered previously all-white reserves the more comfortable I felt in them. In fact I began to think of those spaces as my spaces. I began to eat more and more in white-owned restaurants and less and less in black-owned ones. Because freedom meant I was free to be in and participate in white worlds I practically forgot my own world. Unwittingly I was contributing to its demise. African restaurants closed for lack of African clientele like me. African-owned neighborhood stores did not expand to supermarkets because white-owned store owners with previous segregationist attitudes made it convenient for me to shop in their markets. Slowly (but surely) my interest shifted from African worlds to white worlds. I began to think of white worlds as my worlds and *the real world.* For me the white world was a better world. It had much more than my world. And so, my African world was becoming an alien world for me. Freedom was now being redefined. It now meant living and functioning in white-controlled environments. For me, prior to the desegregation laws, freedom meant living outside of white control.

This shift in physical location and mindset impacted African worlds in America in major ways. Here I offer three.

First, it cost Africans in America the spaces that had given shape and stability to their lives from the time of their enslavement to the end of their conscription. For example, the sacred land that Africans owned in America, and that had enabled Africans to carve out destinies and nourish African-centered perspectives, was significantly diminished or taken from Africans altogether. Indeed, 15 million acres of land Africans owned in America at the beginning of the twentieth century diminished to approximately a third of that amount at the end of the twentieth century. This reduction was due in large measure to disinterest in agricultural lands by Africans because of integrationist pursuits and prospects. That is, hoping to become mainstream actors in the white world Africans in America left their land, belongings, and culture in many cases for a promise land of big city lights and equal opportunities in the 60s and post-60s period. In so doing, deeds and titles to land were left to tax liens and conscription schemes. So, while Africans in America in integration were operating under false nomenclatures, such as "our office," "our company," "our boss," "our property," and so on, southern county administrators and municipalities were busy dishing out their real world to highest bidders in the name of delinquent taxes. Integration meant diminished African ownership of land and real property in America.

Second, it cost Africans in America spaces to showcase self-determination. That is, integration dispossessed Africans of the ability to create and to nurture an African independent future. In particular, Africans in America left their schools, businesses, and institutions for white-owned and operated ones under the behest of an African leadership that strongly believed integration was a "better way." This leadership saw in integration an opportunity for advancement, i.e., an opportunity to prove to white America that Africans had abilities long denied by the white world. Giving up all that makes for community stability, productivity, security and independence, that leadership encouraged Africans to establish new addresses in the white world. It renounced the African world as dated and irrelevant and computed value and meaning only to white measures for black existence. Self-maintaining and self-directing techniques formed and shaped by and for the African world were discarded.

Third, it cost Africans in America their moral voice and moral sense. Having joined the ranks of white ruling-class interest Africans in the majority quit the business of collective justice. Like Europeans in America, Africans also learned to talk about human rights and justice but did not put their rights discussions into practice. This is because integration was designed to wipeout African ways of thinking, believing and doing. For example, unlike popular boxing champion Muhammad Ali, whose keen sense of justice caused him to refuse war duties in Vietnam in the 1960s (and whose integrity cost him his boxing title and fees), Michael Jordan exhibited no such courage in the cause of Indonesian peasant workers in the 1990s. Part and parcel of the integrated system, Jordan would not allow the demoralized circumstances of Indonesia's peasant workers to interfere with his lucrative contract with Nike. He either did not see or would not see that his contract with Nike was being partly financed by underpaid peasant producers of Nike products. Money upstaged morality. Consequently, a more typical African story in America is:

> The Davis family practices what it preaches, instilling in their children the value of investing in products they buy. "Daddy, I like Kool-Aid," Davis' five-year-old daughter once told him. "Can we buy Kool-Aid stock?" His son, who's two and a half, loves Michael Jordan. "He's had three pairs of Air Jordans, but I can tell you, he owns stock in Nike, too.[1]

The above generally describes what has happened to African America after forty years of crossing over into white worlds via integration. In integration personal and individual gains have squashed corporate vision and cancelled justice concerns based on ancestral prodding. Independence has bowed to dependence. As such, the results are not commendable, as I demonstrated in Chapter Six. Is there an alternative to a freedom that after forty years looks like a mistake for a growing number of Africans in America? Is there a way out of *fumbled freedom*? Is there a way out of moral and materialistic slavery?

This chapter will seek to establish – I would say re-establish – a freedom route for Africans in America after more than forty years of fumbled freedom. A modest result should be that other freedom fighters and prophetic visionaries see themselves in the graphics I sketch and find a way to write their histories in other ways also – different from histories of the past 500 years.

The Quest for Freedom in the Key of Africa

In moving towards a description of African freedom in America, perhaps the observation that the great diaspora African scholar W.E.B. DuBois made in his signature work of 1903 regarding the mindset of the African world in America is a good place to begin. Dubois posited that Africans in America possessed double-consciousness or two souls.[2] One soul, he proposed, was shaped and nurtured in the African world and came with enslaved ancestors to America; the other was shaped in America in the process of making Africans Americans.

On one side of the ledger, there was the pressure (self-imposed and imposed by others) on the African in America to become American, i.e., to become Christian (disconnected from Africa's history and heritage) or free in the key of Euro-American aspirations. On the other, there was the pressure to resist Euro-American ways – an obsession of some African enslaved persons to live under the guidance of ancestral memories despite slaveholding pressure to do otherwise. The determination to resist (the issue I am concerned with here) was informed by a peculiar definition of freedom that is African-based. That view of freedom stood opposite to and apart from European cardinal perspectives on freedom that enslaved persons were enticed and pressured to adopt – individual liberty, personal salvation, and economic hegemony.

What is African-based freedom? How did it behave in African worlds and African consciousness in America? These questions will guide our discussion in the remainder of this chapter. Having focused on freedom's manifestation in African worlds, I shall then address a Christian disposition in freedom delineated by Paul. Thereafter, I will use my findings as a basis to describe restructured freedom (liberation) in African worlds in America. I close the curtain with "restructuring directives." An epilogue follows.

Rediscovering the Freedom Tradition of Africa

As oral peoples, traditional African societies passed on history, culture, and customs via aural means. Except for African societies like Egypt, where writing engraved histories and habits for people and centuries unborn (and by Western standards regularized and made that history and tradition less speculative or indefinite), African societies in general were more accustomed to passing along tradition and history by oral means. Storytellers and culture specialists served as timekeepers and monitors of what had been and what was, and as custodians of what was important for generations to come. In these settings the past was antecedent, ancestral, primordial, and programmatic. It gave guidance to the present and directed the present into the future.

As there was not much of a preoccupation with the future (no second chance heaven), the platform of the world (the African world) was life's crucial stage. One was expected to be a good player. To mess up on life's stage was viewed as breach of contract and as a rebellion against the intended order of divine and ancestral ways. Sometimes the cost for messing up yielded community disorders in the form of disease, foreign invasions, and other maladies. A trip to seers or diviners was a necessary step to seek and identify causes for disorder. Once causes were identified, it was thought that if a community so affected followed instructions offered by such specialists for moving beyond infractions (the causes of disorder) to healing and wholeness that community would be restored to normal life. That life (the good life) was life before disgrace, a life of health, good crops, food, harmony, and so on.

The good life was the primordial state, a life of nonruptured existence. One characteristic of that state (and so ancestral) was harmony, the heavenly state in traditional African thinking. To put it another way, individuality or individuated desire was never equated with the heavenly state, for individuated desire, in traditional thinking, meant disruption, pain, and doom. Communality or harmony meant salvation, peace, and the good life. Such was the proper state of existence. Of this state, John S. Mbiti asserts:

> "In traditional society, the individual does not and cannot exist alone except corporately. He owes his

existence to other people, including those of past generations and his contemporaries. He is simply part of the whole.... Whatever happens to the individual happens to the whole group, and whatever happens to the whole happens to the individual. The individual can only say: "I am, because we are; and since we are, therefore I am."[3]

Thus interconnectedness is normative in traditional African thinking and being. Divisiveness or individuated existence is abnormal. Hence African based freedom is harmonious existence (the heavenly state). It is "I am because we are, and we are because I am."

That harmony is the heavenly state (and so primordial) can be gleaned from a West African Yoruba story about how disorder first came into the world. For the Yorubas the Supreme Being, Olorun, devised that all persons at Ile Ife (the Yoruba Garden of Eden in Nigeria) live together as one. Oneness was exhibited in certain features. For example, all Yorubas at Ile Ife were the same size, the same height, the same color, and so on. All Yoruba families had the same number of children, the same amount of land.... Nonetheless, Yorubas became bored and dissatisfied with their sameness. Some wanted to be taller or shorter than others, some wanted more or less land than their neighbors, and some wanted darker or lighter skin than others. Though Olorun objected, as the story goes, the Yorubas insisted that their desires be granted. Through a mediating divinity Olorun reluctantly granted their wishes. Olorun gave Yorubas what they requested, but the variations caused inequality and thereafter infighting and jealousy over which Yoruba had more or less by comparison. Because they had made requests that violated divine and ancestral intentions, Olorun made things worse. In an already confused and disharmonious situation, Olorun gave Yorubas more than they asked for. Olorun gave the Yorubas languages making it impossible for them to communicate with one another. Thus, as the story goes, a good harmonious beginning of equality and bliss turned into unbridled discord and greed, a violation of the ancestral blueprint for proper community life. When individual interests overrode communal interests, the community was destroyed.

In this story the African principle for the good life, "I am because we are," is constitutive for demonstrating how individuals are expected to function in continental African worlds. Freedom meant, "I am because we are." It was that perspective of freedom that seemed more characteristic of African thinking in contexts of the enslaved in America as well. For example, slaves who gained personal or individual freedom by running away in many instances returned to their slaveholding owners – a decision owners found surprising – simply because they (the enslaved) were bothered that they had left their enslaved brothers and sisters behind in bondage. Unlike the thinking of slaveholders, who speculated that runaways returned to atone for violating their trust or to satisfy some biblical directive about the obedience of slaves to masters, returning runaway slaves were more often guided by the principle of interconnectedness. Practically stated: No individual African was free unless all Africans were free.

This principle generated a restless existence for many Africans in America. Barring freedom for all the enslaved, so-called freed slaves either volunteered to rejoin those in slavery, raised funds for manumission of enslaved sisters and brothers, or engaged in plots and schemes to end the enslaving system. The story of Harriet Tubman risking her own life to lead many enslaved persons to freedom and of black abolitionists in the North and the South fighting to free the enslaved by any means necessary are well-known instances of this spirit. Other instances included the refusal of many to accept offers from colonization groups to live as free citizens in Liberia while their enslaved relatives remained behind in bondage and the risks David Walker took in the nineteenth century to ensure that his liberation messages reached the enslaved in the South. In addition, there are the unheralded stories of millions of enslaved Africans who committed themselves to protect each other throughout the period of their ordeal at great danger to life and limb. For these people individual opportunity was governed by corporate responsibility.

Nonetheless, European evangelistic initiatives, with its gospel of rewards and punishments and with emphasis on personal and individuated salvation, weakened the voice of African freedom. Africans who accepted and acted upon the evangelistic voice of freedom were promoted to the ranks of the civilized, to the entrusted, and to the enlightened in slaveholding politics. As converts they were expected to distance themselves from less enlightened, nonaccepting, heathenish sisters and brothers, i.e., those holding African-based ideas about freedom. To show appreciation for their conversion slaveholders tended to reward them with improved positions on the plantation. To show appreciation in kind, these converts often became advocates of personal religion, personal salvation, and personal achievement like their slaveholding masters and mistresses.

After the Civil War the numbers in this group increased. And more revealing is the fact that the African principle of "I am because we are" became less programmatic as evidenced in the titular language, heathen and civilized, the masses and the talented tenth. Today the African situation is more divided. Class matters have divided communities pitting Belshazzar human rights opportunists against non-moneyed masses.

In this environment Africans in America, predisposed to middle-class aspirations, tend to become members and supporters of triumphant Christian movements, because that kind of Christianity represents them best. Typical thinking of this circle is that an increase in individual wealth is a sign of divine favor, hardly an indication of the "I am because we are" principle. But such a disposition is nontraditional for African self-understanding and structuring. Even in Paul, a main staple for anchoring individual advancement to the chagrin of collective responsibility, the African view of freedom finds an ally.

Paul and Freedom

Paul thought of himself as an apostle of freedom, yet he had little if anything to say about freedom as physical deliverance from slaveholding bondage. Paul had a chance to equate freedom with deliverance from slaveholding bondage in his personal letter to Philemon, a slaveholder, but there he advised the return of the slave (Onesimus) to his Christian slaveholder, Philemon.

Christian slaveholders in America lauded Paul for this. They used his Philemon letter to secure their slaveholding investments and to improve their chances for perpetual economic advance at the expense of enslaved Africans. In fact, Philemon as well as Colossians 3:22-25 and Ephesians 6:5-8 (letters attributed to Paul) were seen by slaveholders as clearly, and therefore divinely, supporting slaveholding practices. For that reason many enslaved Africans in America (and their progeny since) looked unfavorably on Paul as a biblical writer. Religionist Howard Thurman reported, for example, that his grandmother – an enslaved African person in America – did not like Paul, because her slaveholding Christian master always made a point of making sure the slaves on his plantation knew Paul's directives regarding their enslavement. She explained:

> Old man McGhee was so mean that he would not let a Negro minister preach to his slaves. Always the white minister used as his text something from Paul. At least three or four times a year he used as a text: 'Slaves, be obedient to them that are your masters... as unto Christ.' Then he would go on to show how it was God's will that we were slaves and how, if we were good and happy slaves, God would bless us. I promised my Maker that if I ever learned to read and if freedom ever came, I would not read that part of the Bible.[4]

However, this same Paul advocated a position on freedom that is in synchrony with African practices in freedom in a continental and diaspora contexts. Galatians exhibits the relationship. Often referred to by commentators as the Christian Magna Carta on freedom, one is surprised to find in Galatians that Paul does not promote a Western, capitalistic view of freedom; freedom in Paul is not thought of in individuated terms. It is not individual liberation or personal salvation – from sin or from any other binding restraint. Rather Paul's freedom is corporately defined, as Paul tends to qualify his discussions on freedom or liberation with plurals. He can say "false believers... who slipped in to spy on the freedom *we* have in Christ Jesus" (Galatians 2:4), or "... *we* are children, not of the slave but of the free woman" (Galatians 4:31), or "For freedom Christ has set *us* free..." (Galatians 5:1a). Furthermore, Paul instructs that the Galatians, once enslaved to "the elemental spirits of the world" (Galatians 4:2) – later defined as "observing special days, and months, and seasons, and years" (Galatians 4:10) – are now manumitted by Jesus, the Son of God. The Galatians are no longer slaves but free persons (Galatians 4:5-7), and as free persons *they* are to stand firm together, never again submitting themselves to slavery (Galatians 5:1b). The Galatians are also warned not to use their freedom selfishly, i.e., for individual opportunity at the expense of the group, "but through love become slaves to one another" (Galatians 5:13). Here then, Paul's musings and reflections on freedom are colored and governed by corporate concerns. Freedom is communal in practice and communally responsible.

The question is – to which community is one to show responsibility to by Paul's standards? Normally to Christians is the answer that comes to mind, except in Galatians the discussion is about *ethnic solitary* and how to win in a world of racial hostility. The point is that Judaizing persons of Galatia, i.e., persons who are promoting Jewish cultural expectations as a plan of salvation for Gentiles, are locked in a battle with Paul about the nature of those expectations. His opponents say that in order for Gentiles to be accepted into the fellowship of Abraham (of Jews), they must obliterate their past and become Jews, i.e., they must be circumcised. In contemporary terms, they were being urged to acculturate and to assimilate to the wishes and traditions of the opposing group. Paul, however, argues otherwise. His ethnic Gentile converts, he argues, do not have to become Jews to live an acceptable life in God. Rather they can be utterly other and different and still be valid.

When they follow their drum beat and live within their on cultural skins, Paul advised, they not only free themselves as a community from the requirements of others for acceptance but connect genuinely with an apostle who is quite "other" too. This apostle (Paul) is an apostle despite a physical disability (Galatians 4:13), a defect that normally disqualifies. Indeed this apostle, in his total carriage, refused to allow the power tactics of one group to alter the ways of the other by insisting that neither he nor the Gentile converts he represented could be saved by the requirements of other human beings. Nor would freedom, properly understood, ever be other than communal in nature. This was Paul's word for the Corinthians also; a community of boasters who did not yet understand that true liberation is communal and corporate.

Freedom, then, in Paul's letter to the Galatians, is ethnic communalism in a society where one ethnic group seeks to enslave another. Freedom is "I am because we are," in situations wherein people are enslaved because of skin color. So ethnic solidarity is encouraged to deter enslavement; when one ethnic group uses another to achieve its goals.

What does this mean for an African middle-class person who has become enslaved to or trapped in this very way? What does it mean for an ethnic group split into class factions, one trapped in a Belshazzar cage of individualistic conduct while the other is trapped in poverty, despair, and degradation and incessantly seeks to be ensnared by that which grips their more able relatives?

Some Implications of Freedom for Africans in America

The above questions go to the heart of the African dilemma in America today, while offering Africans a chance to revisit African views on freedom. Simply put, these questions signify that the solution to the African dilemma in America (one group in subjection to the wishes of another) might mean an exodus from integrated structures and integrated goals, physically and mentally. Of course this suggestion is not revolutionary. It follows the pattern of democratic societies when a particular course proves unproductive. Such societies have elections to determine direction, to discontinue one thing and begin another. In a similar way Paul advised the Galatians to leave the elemental spirits that prevented them from embracing a freedom that was different and salvific. In other words Paul wanted them to forsake slavery – a life of fictitious freedom – and return once again to genuine freedom, i.e., a chance to put into practice perspectives in freedom informed by ancestral traditions. Therefore, separating from that which impedes communal expressions of freedom or that which restrains existence is not only endemic to the Christian tradition; it is also African. It belongs to the ancestral grove.

Here I speak particularly to the African middle class in America and to those of the African world with integrationist aspirations, for it is these classes that are highly motivated to engage in individuated conduct. Indeed it is this interethnic enclave that sets courses for the African world by parading the lanes of ostentatious living while poorer Africans languish in poverty, poor housing, AIDs, starvation, and uncertainty. It is this class that leaves the poor waiting for the moving of the water when its moving requires resources, money, and vision in the modern world. It is this enclave that I herewith challenge to return to the ancestral grove, where they can discover the means for the revival and reconstruction of African worlds.

Returning to the ancestral grove, if I may use a biblical analogy, is the decision to leave the senselessness of Sodom and Gomorrah and to become contributors to the well-being and life of a dying African world. There is a pressing need for people of African descent to stop looking to social science engineers and government planners to speak for them. Instead, people of African descent must become involved in solving the mammoth problems of dispossessed and disinherited Africans who live without benefits from battles they so nobly waged for civil and human rights opportunities in America and for the end of colonialism on the African continent. It is the ethnic duty of middle-class Africans to live without the false markers of social class distinction and integrationist thinking. These Africans are to remind themselves that wounded and abandoned freedom fighters never knew or experienced in America King's beloved community or in Africa Nkrumah's dream of a strong, unified Africa. Literally, returning to ancestral groves means Africans linking hand to hand around the globe to salvage African communities that are too weak to defend against further harm on their own. Thus the ancestors' grove is the re-instituting of a "I am because we are" philosophy in visible ways. Otherwise, Africans, particularly in America, will forever remain in self-inflicted slavery, whether in the trap of the boardroom of the middle class or in the poolroom of the poor.

So what must the African world in America and elsewhere do now? Should diaspora Africans just bid America and other places goodbye and return to ancestral homes? A return would be ideal if the pain of a nonworking relationship is used as a measure, but it would be impractical given the state of things in Africa and the world today. Continental Africa is not owned and operated by Africans just as North America is not owned and operated by Native Americans. The entire African race is now re-enslaved and has been since the 1960s. In plain terms, Africans are once again under the dominance of European and Euro-American control. Indeed, at the very moment Africans became free they were re-interred through integrationist and neo-colonial schemes. Post-apartheid South Africa is the latest to follow this pattern. Its freedom from day one meant a return to apartheid-like conditions in the name of a New South Africa. Freedom means the integration of 25 million blacks into a system controlled by 5 million whites. It is forgiveness without reparation and existence without land.

So how are Africans to survive in strained contexts and in interethnic alienation? What are Africans to do in contexts where nonindigenous views of freedom are pitting African against African in never-ending class and ideological wars? Can an African-based freedom improve African worlds? Here I suggest a two-pronged approach as a treatment for the world-wide African crisis. The first reaches back for the ancestral grove I mentioned above. It calls for a renewal of the prophetic spirit in the African world. Prophecy judges this world and points us to ancestral or proper worlds. The second is what to do with prophetic results and calls for restructured freedom.

Prophetic Speaking in Africa America

Prophetic speaking is a form of speech that seeks to arrest drifting societies, reconnecting them to charter meanings. As such prophetic speaking is roots speech.

Prophetic speaking is likely to occur in contexts where societies substitute charter ideas for lesser or twisted ones and where societies are headed for destruction. As such it is salvific in tone. It tells of ancestral displeasure with a human circumstance that stands in need of correction. It presumes that corrections based on ancestral prodding can save a society from certain doom. Thus prophetic speaking portends to be truth speaking for good results. In the language of African ancestors it is speaking "the unadulterated truth," particularly to situations where injustice reigns and where straight talk about truth is missing.

However, prophetic speaking – main course speech in African worlds a short time ago – is hardly a staple of African rhetoric today. Africans in America seldom experience it, and so the ancestral voice goes unheard and unknown. And why is this? It is because of a patron-client system in which Africans in America have accepted and participated in uncritically since the 1960s. It is a system informed by an integrationist philosophy, American style. Its end product is an enslaved African middle class that parades around proudly in the name of progress but has little knowledge of what progress means in ancestral terms.

So how can there be an ancestral voice when individualism and greed have for more than forty years upstaged that voice? I believe there can be a voice, but its revival will depend on memory. Memory can lead back to primordial constructs and primordial constructs (the ancestral world) can lead forward to re-envisioning and envisioning, especially when people recognize where they have been, where they currently are, and where they ought to be.[5]

Memory, i.e., the oral tradition, teaches that before integration Africans worlds in America thrived. Segregated, Africans in America created worlds based on self-reliance and communal sharing as virtues. They owned and operated insurance companies, businesses, farms, independent schools, hospitals, hotels, restaurants, and much more. While money did not grow on trees, so to speak, compassion did for Africans what money could not. Without government-sponsored welfare and goodwill from the larger society, Africans in America invented welfare programs through networks of communal sharing. They pooled their resources to bury the dead and keep their communities afloat. They built colleges and churches, and by such means educated their own children and honed ancestral connections. In short, they made available to their progeny a distinct African way: love and kindness for each other in an unfriendly world.

Integration killed all that. Out of a montage of interdependency grew indebtedness to and dependency on a world that muted African ingenuity. That world birthed a new voice. It was not shaped by prophetic instructions of the ancestors, but by voices of enslaved and suppressed beings. Thus the riveting voice of a Martin Luther King challenging white America to do justice based on the prophet Micah – "Let justice roll down like mighty waters and righteous like a mighty stream" – in the 1950s and 60s fell silent in the 1980s and 90s. By then focusing on mainstream desire had turned a mighty stream of ancestral ways into intermittent drips. This was because what the prophet decried as offensive and unjust had become an African way in the hall of integration. Memories of primordial constructs and directions had become muddled. The victim had become victimizer because primordial wells were covered.

Traditionally, the African in America looked to her or his preacher to offer prophetic instructions when contrary winds blew over their worlds. Indeed the preacher was viewed as an ancestral medium, a primordial moral mouthpiece through which the Divine spoke and gave judgements. The preacher was a prophet. She or he stood apart from the trappings and ways of the world and was therefore in position to challenge human practices that were contrary to God's way. To paraphrase Dr. Gardner C. Taylor, the African preacher was God's defense attorney.

As a prophet the preacher thought of herself or himself as commissioned by and answerable to divine directions alone; but the integrationist movement in the 1960s changed that. Deciding to become a chief promoter of integrationist strategies, the African preacher switched from spokesperson for divine justice to spokesperson for mainstream interests. Rather than getting the message from beyond to critique what is as the ancestors and the biblical Amos had done in the past, the integrationist African preacher turned to interracial engagements and committees for pulpit instructions and assignments. As a result, the rhetorical "thus says the Lord" so prevalent among African preachers in the preintegration period, became negotiated settlements thereafter. Indeed, the African preacher became preoccupied with "not offending the white brethren." As a consequence the African preacher developed spiritual asthma. Sermons became less critical of the ways of white folk and the mistakes of black folk. Sadly, preaching turned into a celebration of integrationist victories with the preacher as cheerleader.

Thus the African preacher, because of her or his uncritical embrace of European values in America, showed signs of amnesia vis-à-vis the preacher's traditional function. This led the African religious community in America away from its historic role – as protector and guardian of justice for African and other oppressed people in America. Rather than modeling the spiritual and just life, it became a harbinger of unjust reminders. Indeed, it became an exhibit station of capitalism – costly goods, expensive automobiles, clothing, expensive jewelry, frivolous behavior, and crass inequities. It stopped saying that the love of money is the root of evil. Instead, it sanctioned money and the pursuit of money as a heavenly goal. Thus abrogating its traditional role, the African religious community (the African church in America) by the 80s and 90s became Eurocentric – not Christocentric, Afrocentric, or anthropocentric.

Behind the loss of memory and silence of the African preacher and African church today stands the ringing ancestral voices of Nat Turner, David Walker, *Sojourner Truth*, Henry Highland Garnet, Alexander Crummell, Frederick Douglass, Henry McNeal Turner, Malcolm X, Angela Davis, Fanny Lou Hammer, and a host of lesser-noted individuals. Such prophetic voices are reminders of times when African leaders were fearless confessors and visionaries. They are also reminders of times when the prophetic African voice was transnational in range, speaking on domestic as well as foreign issues. For example, Martin Luther King and Muhammad Ali spoke out against America's involvement in Vietnam. Fannie Lou Hamer challenged white America on politics and power. Frederick Douglass told America in 1852 that its Fourth of July celebration was a sham when enslavement of Africans in America hung like a threatening cloud over the nation. David Walker spoke of a regrettable day for slaveholders. Henry Highland Garnet called for an armed rebellion against slaveholders.

If one such voice existed in African worlds today, it would speak resoundingly about a different approach to the African dilemma in America and in the world. Perhaps it would insist that continental African leaders (especially warmongers) end strife and blood baths, and cease creating refugee camps of displaced people. Perhaps it would insist that Africans put an end to slavery in African lands. It would insist that the poor in African worlds be liberated from poverty, disease, injustice, and death. It would insist that the rich and able improve conditions of the poor by downsizing their ostentatious holdings so that the masses share in the fruits of the good earth as humans in the image of the Divine. Indeed, the prophetic ancestral voice would call for a revival of life and meaning based on primordial principles and terms.

The prophetic voice would address America directly, calling attention to two long-standing cases of American involvement. One is the Palestinian dilemma. Reports are that there were 6.8 million Palestinians in 1996. At the time of *al-Nakbah* – what Palestinians call the destruction of their society and the "dispossession, dispersal and destitution" of their people by Israel and its allies in 1947-48 to make possible "a Jewish state without indigenous Arab Palestinians" – approximately 900,000 Palestinians lived in what is now Israel.[6] According to statistics, "750,000 to 800,000 of those became refugees" and were dispersed to the "West Bank, the Gaza Strip, and to neighboring Arab countries."[7] The Middle East writer-historian Farsoum notes:

> The bulk of the 1948 Palestinians fled their homes, villages, and land primarily because of the mortal fear created by the systematic terror campaigns conducted by the Israeli State forces. Even as they took flight, however, there was never a question of return: It was always a matter of when and how, not whether they would return. As time went on and the tragedies accumulated, the mystique of "the return" became even stronger. In many a Palestinian home in the diaspora, families display olive wood carvings or framed needlework pictures with the words "Innana raji`oun or 'Innana `ai'-doun" (We shall return).[8]

On the matter of Palestinians returning to Palestine, Israel and the world must realize after fifty years of fighting that there will be no real peace in the Middle East until Palestinian rights are recognized and respected. Israel must realize that oppressed people force their oppressors to hear them in one form or another and that it should consider this in light of its own history in biblical and contemporary times. Indeed, the ancient Israelites agitated and fought the ancient Egyptians until they were liberated from slavery. The same held true in the time of Judas Maccabeus and his followers in the second century B.C.E. Neither group would retreat until liberation was achieved and justice established. It is a long-standing human principle that justice is the price one pays for peace.

Since biblical times Jewish people have known and suffered many tragedies. Perhaps the one that is most memorable and widely known is the holocaust tragedy of the 1940s. The world should never forget the millions of Jews who suffered and died in concentration camps. In that tragedy alone Jews came to know the depths of suffering and therefore should not find it difficult to empathize with the sufferings of others. In fact the moral and spiritual history of Jews and Judaism, especially the urgings of the prophets, disallowed oppression altogether. It was the prophet Micah who pleaded with the nation to seek justice. I do not think that it is unsound to say in reading the record on Judaism that Yahweh demands justice.

That Yahweh demands it and rewards pursuers of it is the poignant message of Passover, a liberation experience that is larger than ethnicity. Here I would suggest that freedom should never mean opportunistic behavior. Peace comes only after justice is served; when the rights of the abused are recognized and honored.

The other long-standing case that begs for a prophetic voice lies within American borders. It is the Native American problem created by European conquistadors centuries ago. While Africans regrettably came to America as slaves, Jews and others suffered the European holocaust, and Palestinians were dispossessed and then dispersed from their land for more than fifty years, the Native American story of unjust treatment is far more gripping and tragic. Nations of Native American peoples were wiped off the face of the earth simply because of the greed and trickery of European settlers and colonizers. There are reports that when Christopher Columbus came to the island of Hispaniola in 1492 he and his crew were the welcomed guests of 250,000 Indians. He organized a colony there in 1494, and by 1515 there were "seventeen Spanish towns on the inland; (and) mines were being worked... all by the labor of enslaved Indians, the same people who had welcomed Columbus so innocently on his voyage discovery."[9] By 1515, the 250,000 Indians Columbus met in 1492 had been reduced to 14,000, and not long thereafter the entire population was extinct.[10]

The welcome-enslave-extinction scheme is an old one in the Americas – assisted by European diseases and bellicose conduct.[11] Placed atop this pattern in North America was the government's Indian Removal Act of 1830, a scorched-earth policy in America, legislated to make room for an increasing European population of settlers. Signed by President Andrew Jackson, this act essentially sought to erase Native Americans from the American landscape by deporting them from the East to the West like criminals in their own land. Western expansionism in search of gold only added to their miseries. In short, Native Americans lost their land, their homes, and their lives because of the greed of interlopers.

The Native American issue is the grievous sin for which whites in America have yet to properly atone. The sad irony is that America has attempted to compensate, in one form or another, all other groups it has wronged except the indigenous peoples. Justice for them should now be a high priority. Native Americans should be allowed to state the compensatory price no matter how high it might be. This should be a first order of business of the new century; otherwise, in prophetic speech, this land will know no peace.

European descendents in America will have to admit in the face of peace that it has committed no greater crime than the one it committed against indigenous peoples of America. The crime against Africans was grave – more than 200 years of slavery, millions killed, and about eighty years of segregation – but the one against America's natives is more heinous. In each of the other cases, the people enslaved or oppressed eventually broke through to life and freedom after protracted struggles. This was also the case in Asian and in continental African worlds in the fight for freedom from colonial oppression in the 1950s and 60s; hardly any Native Americans have witnessed those worldwide winds of liberation and freedom. Most had been silenced by death. The rest stood on the landscape of the forgotten, tucked out of sight and out of mind, in alleys of cities and on reservations, contending with problems of alcoholism and with a suicide rate higher than any ethnic group in America. Few are their voices for justice now; yet, in the spirit of prophecy, these few are to be recognized and people of good will and justice are to be encouraged to join hands with them in quest for a final resolution to their problem.

Prophetic Restructuring in Africa America

If speaking prophetically assumes that a wrong done needs to be righted, as I assume here, then the flip side of prophecy portends deliverance, i.e., the life that fulfills ancestral expectations. In that way prophecy is safeguarded from becoming no more than negative remarks about questionable lifestyles of people and nations. It becomes also a word about repentance in real terms. Here repentance is more than a verbalization of remorse and sorrow for deeds done in the past. It is a radical shift of direction that becomes demonstrable in future actions, selections, and duties towards those who have been wronged. The biblical prophet Amos exhibits this spirit:

> On that day, says the Lord God, I will make the sun go down at noon, and darken the earth in broad daylight. I will turn your feast into mourning, and all your songs into lamentations; I will bring sackcloth on all loins, and baldness on every head; I will make it like the mourning of an only son, and the end of it is like a bitter day. [Amos 8:9-10, NRSV]

These doom-filled words of Amos are only the first base of prophecy. Amos went on to prophecy's second (and most important) base. Indeed, the people whom he had condemned a little while before were now called to a reconfigured existence based on an ancestral outlook. Amos alludes to it as follows:

... the mountains shall drip sweet wine, and all the

hills shall flow with it. I will restore the fortunes of
Israel, and they shall rebuild the ruined cities and
inhabit them; they shall plant vineyards and drink
their wine and they shall make gardens and eat their
fruit. I will plant them upon their land and they
shall never again be plucked up of the land that I
have given them, says the Lord your God. [Amos
9:13b-15, NRSV].

Thus true prophecy is re-creation. It presages restored existence. The world as it once was literally returning to earth is
its true goal.

So what does this mean for African existence in America
and elsewhere? It means that freedom must be redefined as
restored existence. It means to come back, not to go away.
Such freedom means deliverance from death to life; from frag-
ile existence to wholeness. It is the state wherein people imagine the unimaginable, indeed a New World that is quite old.
It is existence not fashioned out of individuality but communality. In Western contexts it is the oppressed released from
imperialist demands and colonizing behavior to make a world
in the image of their ancestral intentions.

How would this appear in real terms? The directives below
attempt to describe how this might appear among Africans in
America, presupposing that prophetic thinking and existing by
nature necessarily relate to charter issues. The points delineated assume the willingness of Africans in America to do
penance for deep sins of class and economic division – part of
integration's yield – that have festered in African communities since the 1960s. They anticipate that Africans in America
will join hands, immediately take up the work of their own liberation, and no longer look to others to solve problematic
issues that can only be remedied by ancestral directives.
Furthermore, they assume that Africans in America admit to
a major mistake – more than forty years of misery and self-
destruction under integrationist directives and schemes. Thus,
I offer the following seven directives for African redemption
in America:

Directive 1. **Spiritual Leadership**

Africans in America must rethink and reconsider the role religion has played in African life from the time of slavery until the present. Their current understanding of religion is basically warmed over bread from the religious ovens of Europe. Not only have current African structures in religion emanated from Europeans, they were honed in Europe to institutionalize European interests at home (in Europe) and to foster European interests abroad. What I mean is that these mission-minded configurations were designed to keep Africans subservient to European interests. Therefore, Africans in America must not only retire these systems (remember the discussion of Galatians above); they must work out the specifics of a system that is faithful to ancestral aims.

Africans must insist that their priests and priestesses promote views of religion chiseled out of prophetic circles of thinking and anchored in ancestral philosophy. Dealing as traditionally they do with life and death, this class of religionists – priests and priestesses – must be trained in institutions promoting African salvation. They must learn and study the concerns of the people in depth as well as the concerns of other oppressed peoples. I say this because freedom demands it.

The focus of priestly study must be the people's issues, not ruling-class, Eurocentric ones as is widely the custom in theological studies in African worlds today. This is important because people, those really concerned about freedom and how to maintain it under oppressive conditions, do not allow those who oppress them to determine their religious and doctrinal menus. In the interest of justice and wisdom they seek spiritual guidance from their own sages and instructors. Elijah's spirit was certainly transferred to Elisha.

Directive 2. **Prodigal Drifters**

African parishioners in America have joined white churches in great numbers in fulfillment of the promises of integration over the last forty years. These are called multi-ethnic or multiracial churches, usually led by a white pastor.

Perhaps this is ideal but I argue that African problems in the world are African-created and that integration created much that is wrong with the black world today. For that reason those who have put their energies in multiracial churches might do well to consider that the energies placed there could benefit a world that is almost destroyed.

These Africans should consider returning to ancestral centers of spirituality. They must come to see that multiracial structures in religion by constitution cannot service the all-consuming dangers faced by Africans in America today. These structures and their doctrinal presuppositions cannot and do not promote the ways of the African freedom tradition. Furthermore, they rob Africans in particular of tithes, offerings, talents, and other gifts that could be put to good use in restoring African worlds to health and vitality.

Prodigal drifters might consider the following: Ancestral freedom means departing from structures and contexts that retreats from proper African life. The proper life is a life of *full being* in the church and the world. It is the life of African communal existence.

Directive 3. **Institutions of Higher Education**

African universities, colleges, and schools in America and elsewhere must be strengthened. Since the 1960s African institutions of higher learning have progressively weakened or disappeared. In America one reason for this diminution is that integration lured the best students of the African community to colleges and universities previously reserved for whites only. Students from previously "white only" institutions are likely to become ardent supporters of the institutions from which they graduate. However, those schools have and do survive without financial contributions from their African graduates. Traditional African schools cannot.

This may seem a bit unpatriotic to some, however blacks and whites in America already know that U.S. taxpayers contribute handsome annual sums in support of public institutions of higher learning. Yet, in America, tax revenue is unequally distributed among historically African and non-

African (white) institutions. Racism demands it.

A case in point is the state of Virginia: A disproportion-ate amount of taxpayer dollars for publicly sponsored educa-tion is allocated to traditionally white commonwealth institutions, thus making them top rated among Virginia's colleges and universities. A pittance, by comparison, is allo-cated to traditionally African colleges and universities. The result is that one school has enormous resources and is white; the other has little and is black. One (white) gets better; the other (black) gets worse. One lures Africans to improve their position in the white world; the other does not. In fact, Africans disregard the latter because integrationist training teaches that the white world is the place to be. It has what the black world needs.

Africans in America should no longer submit to the view that life's chances can only be improved upon in white-dom-inated educational circles. Such sinister and selfish persuasions diminish African importance in the world; for example, too many Africans in America already operate on the premise that working in an African institution in America after graduating from a white one constitutes downward mobility or a failure in career goals. The situation also works in reverse: Too many Africans view a move from the African to the white world as a promotion or a leg up in life.

When such attitudes prevail, i.e., when African employ-ment in the white world is equated with success and progress, African institutions suffer. Such thinking also causes Africans to shy away from working on African issues, as did their ances-tors – the freedom-loving George Washington Carver, Booker T. Washington, Mary McCleod Bethune, and others – before freedom became integration. They believed that one did not go to school to get a job in another's world. One went to school to do a job in or for the African world.

Success for these ancestors was working on African issues. In that light my hope, then, is that each person of African decent will step up, adopt an African college or university in America or elsewhere, and financially support it regardless of his or her personal or academic affiliation with that institution.

Also, each African should choose an African issue and work on it. Each would do well to adopt the attitude of the African ancestor who helped to make Tuskegee University what it is today by contributing six eggs. Each African should be imbued with the spirit of Oseola McCarty (ninety-one years old in 1998 but now deceased) of Hattiesburg, Mississippi, who did laundry work her entire life and gave the University of Southern Mississippi $150,000 "because she wants other blacks to have a better life."[12] I can only hope that the next time a gift of that magnitude is given the donor could find an African private institution of higher education deserving the honor.

The decision of Oseola McCarty to fund scholarships for black students matriculating at a predominately Euro-American institution of higher education is an important announcement to African institutions. African institutions of higher education must show that they deserve such gifts by structuring a curriculum suitable to the needs and strategies of African communities. The old guardians of African higher education must "get with it" or get out of the business. They must realize that they have too often kept African communities from truly being educated by insisting on the status quo. They must realize that Africans have a right to develop educational systems that work for them, and that relate to clear mandates of African communities. Too often the situation has been the reverse: African institutions have been feeders of systems that oppress African communities.

The curriculum of African institutions should reflect Africanized values, i.e., the focus should not be on the diminution of life but on its restoration and continuance. African people must be trained to work on subjects that benefit African lives and communities. The under-girding philosophy of all African institutions should be educating students to make a positive difference in African worlds and worlds of the oppressed.

The end of education is liberation. All persons of African descent should become involved in and benefit from African higher education initiatives. African educational delivery systems should press at all times to focus on the people's issues and needs. They should systematically educate the people on health issues, community issues, religious issues, social issues, political issues, business issues, economic issues, world issues, and so on. They should teach the trades – brick masonry, carpentry, construction and engineering, plumbing, processing of foods, indeed all that pertains to wellbeing in the world.

Directive 4. **Interethnic Relationships**

Africans must once again identify the practices that make groups strong and those that weaken them. To be noted is the fact that Africans in America survived slavery and segregation for centuries because of their strong connections with one another, i.e., they thought of themselves in familial terms, as brothers and sisters, when faced with problems generated by racist conduct in America. Their clarity on that point created a resolve among them to work together for survival. Knowing what the issue was they fought as a group to defeat it. However, since the 1970s Africans in America have become unfocused due to integrationist habits. They now argue about status and class. As a result there are middle-class and underclass divisive camps in the African world in America and elsewhere. And intrapersonal scrimmages among these divisions have left unchecked the growth of what W.E.B. Dubois described a century ago as America's problem – the race problem. Consequently, an ever-widening chasm now exists among Africans in America and between Africans in America and Africans elsewhere, a chasm that will become wider in the future because of economic disparity between those with and those without in both contexts. Special interest division will grow if not checked. For that reason walls that separate African from African should be torn down through concerted, orchestrated efforts.

African peoples must see that their plight is the same the world over – too much poverty, foreign controllers, and disregard for African particulars. Amadou Diallo (murdered by New York police in 1999) is no different from Rodney King (almost beaten to death by Los Angeles police earlier on).

The six-eggs-African woman was no different from Booker T. Washington, the president and founding member of Tuskegee University in Alabama. All are no more or no less than sisters and brothers with different assignments working on the same project – African survival and liberation.

Directive 5. Farms and Cooperatives

People of African descent the world over (in Africa and in the diaspora) turned away from farming in droves during the freedom movement of the 1950s and 60s. I need not rehash detailed reasons for this (e.g., a switch from a production to a service economy, or the allurements of bright lights in cities), but the fact remains that African land lies fallow in continental and diaspora contexts. Africans in both contexts beg others for food.

On the continent there is plenty of open land for farming. In America there is still open land owned by Africans, but too many Africans in America have virtually left bread for their tables as a project for others. Africans in America are not even producing food on a small scale; yet hunger and joblessness abound in African worlds.

Africans in America and on the continent should once again become food growers, producers, and controllers like their ancestors. On a small scale African people can work themselves out of the hole of food dependency. As growers, producers, and controllers they could foster cooperatives like other ethnic groups. All Africans could become sponsors for the wellbeing of one another. It is a great sin to treat this issue otherwise.

Directive 6. Businesses and Banks

In the last thirty-five plus years African businesses in America have steadily disappeared from the landscape. On the continent, such groups as the IMF, the World Bank, and foreign non-African investors virtually control Africa's business potential. This is not to say that Africa is totally controlled by foreign interests. Rather the intent is to sound the alarm that Africans are not main players even in predominately African contexts. Today, for example, Africans in America play large roles in arts entertainment. However, African-owned main staple Africans businesses, such as community stores, that should have become chain stores during civil rights times, were abandoned for a "better chance" in white-owned grocery stores. When Africans got off the bus in Montgomery, Alabama, in 1954, they should have sought a better ride on their own buses. This did not happen, because progress was viewed in the African world in America as sitting on front seats of white-owned buses.

The point here is that Africans must make concerted and studied efforts to put Africans to work via businesses and jobs they create. Clothes and shoes must be worn, food must be produced and consumed, houses must be built and renovated, cars must be manufactured and repaired, and suppliers must meet the needs of consumers.

Africans must empower their current banking institutions and create others as needs arise. Then they must monitor their banking habits. Reports show that the total income for Africans in North America is currently more than $450 billion a year. With that kind of income Africans of North America cannot be said to be financially weak. Africans are just a sector of the population that does not know what to do with money.

Africans need to understand that money is not ability in and of itself. The right use of money is. Thus Africans in North America should gather their money from the paths of wrongful use, pool it, and use it wisely in a country with little compassion for frivolous people. The right use of money can redeem a dysfunctional situation. Blight can be turned into beauty; and sorrows can turn into joy with wise stewardship of resources.

Directive 7. Conventions

Every group needs to consult about issues that affect the group in general. In Africa America, the need to consult regularly and systematically is unquestionable. However, it is troubling that African meetings for consultation purposes in

America are often a misdirection of energy and resources. Too often Africans meet in great numbers for something that a few representatives could handle on behalf of the rest. The fact is that serious work cannot be done when convention-eers are not focused and their numbers are too large. Indeed, a group can become unfocused when numbers become more important than a well-defined purpose. Thus African con-ventioneers must admit that convention meeting is not always a convention meeting. If a convention meeting by definition is one that is designed to focus on the real issues of people (I cannot think of a convention that would be otherwise), then it should not be a time of mass ineptitude, eating, greeting, and venting.

I need not say that African representatives of the people waste too much money on unhelpful things in the name of convention. The money these representatives spend at these conventions (e.g., for room and board, for transportation to convention sites, for food and purchases) could be used more wisely. It is a fact: Some African conventioneers have been known to dump as much as $20 million into the laps of white America (something white America has never dropped in black laps) but not an ounce of good is gathered among the delegates and attendees for African liberation and improve-ment. A different approach with the same $20 million could have translated into hotels and lodges owned and operated by African people, the proceeds of which could help to empower the poor as well as other projects.

Africans in America should not want to be like whites at this point. Being far away from slavery and legalized segre-gation, they should want to do things in their own way and so distinguish themselves again as a unique and powerful peo-ple. Nevertheless, any group can learn a thing or two from other groups. In this regard whites in America may have a lot to teach Africans in America about spending money.

Notes

1. *Black Enterprise* (September 1998): 29/2:49.
2. W.E.B. Dubois, *The Souls of Black Folk*, p. 3.

3. John S. Mbiti, *African Religions and Philosophy* (Garden City, New York: Doubleday and Company, 1970), p. 141.

4. Howard Thurman, *Jesus and the Disinherited* (New York and Nashville: Abingdon-Cokesbury, 1949), pp. 30-31.

5. Professor Orlando Patterson thinks that the African situation in America is much better for Africans than I. He thinks Africans in America have made tremendous progress under integration. See his *The Ordeal of Integration* (1997), especially pp. 17-27 and 171-203.

6. See Samih K Farsoun with Christina E. Zacharia, *Palestine and the Palestinians* (Boulder, Colorado: Westview Press, 1997), p. 123.

7. Ibid.

8. Ibid., p. 127.

9. Angie Debo, *The History of the Indians of the United States* (Norman, Oklahoma: University of Oklahoma Press, 1970), p. 20.

10. Ibid.

11. See Russell Thornton, *The Cherokees: A Population History* (Lincoln and London: University of Nebraska Press, 1990).

12. *Jet* (August 28, 1995): 88/12: 12-13.

Epilogue

The seven directives offered, in concluding Chapter Seven, are simply pointers to African freedom and liberation in the world, and as such they are not comprehensive. Left unstated are directives on family and social issues and a host of others, such as single parent households and prison conditions, which Africans everywhere face, sort out, and grapple with daily. [As my readers you are encouraged add to this list. My primary interest is that you do so and do it quickly, since our ultimate aim here is to draw continental and diaspora Africans away from self-destructive behaviors – from dependency on others – and to move both towards liberation and restoration befitting the ways of ancestors.] I chose them only to indicate the general direction Africans might take if the classic or ancestral notion of freedom is ever to be realized and lived out in African worlds again. My view is that they show that freedom is always redemptive and salvific. I might hasten to say that this does not mean that it is the mass suicide we witnessed in Uganda in the millennium year 2000. That event was a reflection of much that has gone wrong in African thinking. Too many Africans on the continent and in the diaspora practice views of freedom based on poppycock notions that are paraded about as evangelistic truths. This is anti-African freedom. This is a strange and harmful freedom. It means that the African world has work to do. It must redefine its tradition of freedom; it must return to ancestral ways. My seven directives are a challenge towards that end.

It is my hope that African people, as oppressed exiles in the diaspora and as suppressed and oppressed persons on the continent, will return to a common life and gather from the wells of ancestral dreams and styles the true way of African freedom, responsibility, and liberation. I yearn to see freedom practiced in the ancestral style after more than 500 years of mistakes. As such my seven suggestions define liberation not as a departure from African worlds but as a re-entry into that which makes African freedom different from Western notions of freedom and democracy. I believe these suggestions show that freedom means sticking together in a world full of hostility and contempt for people with a different history.

I have spoken of liberation here as a nationalist exodus. A nationalist call for me is not a call for Africans in the Americas and in other diaspora contexts to return to the continent; nor is it a call for Africans on the continent to leave Africa for America or for other places. These days the grass is not greener on the other side of the fence. Rather it is a call for an African divorce from exploitation philosophy and integrationist ways promoted by those with one-world plans. Such plans have disfigured Africa's best sense of freedom and justice.

As taxpayers in North America Africans in America are due certain benefits as U.S. citizens and therefore should not be viewed as parasites on the system when getting their due. To be sure, Africans are not the champions of America's system of handouts. Those with real wealth are leaders of that class. Nevertheless, Africans in America must not gloat about this. Rather they must live from now on as though the system is damaging to their own abilities and best interests. In that demeanor may ties and interconnectedness abound. Freedom is the rich and the poor, the able and the disable of the African world walking together the rest of the way.

African ancestors used to say that when they walked

together – not when we walk apart – the world could not do them harm. One of Africa's great ancestors from slavery in America, Aunt Shady Anne Sutton, viewed this walking together as a coat of protection against hurt:

> Now, back there in slavery time, us didn't have no power of protection, and God knowed it, and put us under watch-care. Rattlesnakes never bit no colored folks until four years after freedom was declared. That was to give us time to learn and to know.[1]

Is there any truth in what this great ancestor said? I think so.

It is my belief that by the year 2022 Africans the world over can become less snake-bitten than they are now. By then, if Africans unite to envision freedom in collective terms, Africans would no longer need to depend on systems that are tired of lending support. Rather than being custodians of bailouts and handouts, Africans could become 75 percent responsible for their existence in America and in the world within 20 years. Paradigms abound in history of other ethnic and national groups that overcame far more than African people with much less. I, too, believe anything is possible when people work together. In this regard, Africans would do well never to forget the attitude that ancestor Booker T. Washington recorded in his *Up from Slavery* (1901), when things were extremely difficult in the early years of the Tuskegee project. Faced with no room to house an increasing student population at Tuskegee, Washington planned a mammoth housing project without as much as a single dime to begin it:

> After having had a preliminary sketch of the needed building made, we found that it would cost about ten thousand dollars. We had no money whatever with which to begin; still we decided to give the needed building a name. We knew we could name

it, even though we were in doubt about our ability to secure the means for its construction.[2]

The point is this: Washington was bold enough to name the future. How unique that was! *Naming the future is the future*. The hall was built. Alabama Hall was built because Washington and his community thought it could be done. They thought that Africans in America could move beyond slavery into a world shaped by African hands and heads for the good of African people and for the good of a world badly in need of a fresh start. The African world can still do that.

Epilogue

1. Langston Hughes and Arna Bontemps (eds.), *The Book of Negro Folklore* (New York: Dodd, Mead & Company, 1958), p. 96.
2. Booker T. Washington, *Up from Slavery*, p. 125.

Selected Bibliography

Ayittey, George N. *Africa in Chaos*. New York: St. Martin's Press, 1998.

Bodansky, Yossef. *Bin Laden: The Man Who Declared War on America*. Rocklin: Prima Publishing, 1999.

Castaneda, Jorge G. *The Mexican Shock: Its Meaning for the US*. New York: The New Press, 1995.

Davidson, Basil. *The Black Man's Burden-Africa and the Curse of the Nation-State*. New York: Random House, 1992.

Debo, Angie. *The History of the Indians of the United States*. Norman: University of Oklahoma Press, 1970.

Dubois, W.E.B. *The Souls of Black Folk*. Reprint, New York: The Blue Heron Press, 1953.

Farsoun, Samih K. with Christina E. Zacharia, *Palestine and the Palestinians*. Boulder: Westview Press, 1997.

Frankfort, Henri. *Ancient Egyptian Religion*. NewYork: Columbia University Press, 1948.

Fuentes, Carlos. *A New Time for Mexico*. Berkeley and Los Angeles: University of California Press, 1997.

Herrnstein, Richard J., and Charles Murray. *The Bell Curve: Intelligence and Class Structure in American Life*. New York: The Free Press, 1994.

Herskovits, Melville J. *The Myth of the Negro Past*. Boston: Beacon Press, 1958. Reprint, Gloucester: Peter Smith, 1970.

Hughes, Langston and Arna Bontemps, eds. *The Book of Negro Folklore*. New York: Dodd, Mead & Company, 1958.

Jordan, Winthrop D. *White Over Black: American Attitudes Toward the Negro, 1550-1812*. Chapel Hill: The University of North Carolina Press, 1968.

Kenyatta, Jomo. *Facing Mount Kenya*. New York: Vintage Books, 1965.

King, Martin Luther, Jr. *Where Do We Go From Here: Chaos or Community?*. Boston: Beacon Press, 1967.

Mbiti, John S. *African Religions and Philosophy*. New York: Doubleday, 1969.

Michel, Lou and Dan Herbeck. *American Terrorist: Timothy McVeigh & the Oklahoma City Bombing*. New York: HarperCollins, 2001.

Oliver, Melvin H. and Thomas M. Shapiro. *Black Wealth/White Wealth: A Perspective on Racial Inequality*. New York and London: Routledge, 1995.

Patterson, Orlando. *Freedom: Freedom in the Making of Western Culture.* San
Francisco: HarperCollins Publishers, 1991.

————. *The Ordeal of Integration: Progress and Resentment in America's
"Racial" Crisis.* Washington: Civitas/Counterpoint, 1997.

Richburg, Keith B. *Out of America: A Black Man Confronts Africa.* New
York: Harcourt Brace, 1998.

Smiley, Tavis, ed. *How to Make Black America Better.* New York: Random
House, 2001.

Snowden, Frank M., Jr. *Blacks in Antiquity: Ethiopians in the Greco-Roman
Experience.* Cambridge: The Belknap Press of Harvard University Press,
1970.

Thornton, Russell. *The Cherokees: A Population History.* Lincoln and
London: University of Nebraska Press, 1990.

Thurman, Howard. *Jesus and the Disinherited.* New York and Nashville:
Abingdon-Cokesbury, 1949.

Washington, Booker T. *Up from Slavery.* New York: Doubleday and
Company, 1901.

West, Cornel. *Race Matters.* Boston: Beacon Press, 1993.

Wilson, William Julius. *The Truly Disadvantaged: The Inner City, the
Underclass and Public Policy.* Chicago and London: The University of
Chicago Press, 1987.

————. *When Work Disappears: The World of the New Urban Poor.* New
York: Vintage Books, 1996.

Womack, John, Jr. *Zapata and the Mexican Revolution.* New York: Random
House, 1968.

Woodson, Carter G. *The History of the Negro Church*, 3rd ed. Washington:
The Associated Publishers, 1972.

————. *The Mis-Education of the Negro.* Washington: Associated
Publishers, 1933. Reprint, Trenton: African World Press, 1990.

NEWSPAPERS AND JOURNALS

USA Today
World Press Review
Charlotte Observer
U.S. News and World Report
Black Enterprise
Jet

INTERNET SOURCES

The New York Times
African Perspective
CNN

Index

INDEX OF BIBLICAL AND EXTRABIBLICAL SOURCES